Soup Maker Recipe Book

The Ultimate Soup Maker Cookbook with Over 101 Quick & Delicious Recipes with Easy to Follow Instructions. Suitable for all Soup Makers. (Desserts & Snacks Included)

Sarah Jones

Table of Contents

INTRODUCTION

This book celebrates the world of soup making whether it is a starter to a full meal or a lunchtime meal in itself. All over the world chefs have created soups in many different consistencies and flavours. Some are thin like consommé, with a clear, delicate colour and a distinct meat flavour. Others are thick, warm and full of meat chunks, such as the traditional broth found in Ireland and Scotland. Spicy soups from Asia give a warm taste to the tongue on chilly winter days. The wonderful thing about soup is that when you eat it in different seasons, you can celebrate the vegetables or fruit that are in season, in both winter and summer. This book will share recipes and tips on how to make soup the easy way, using a soup maker. First, let's take a look at the history of soup-making, so you can decide how to use your soup-making machine to suit your taste and the season.

The history of soup making

Many of us are familiar with tins of soup found stacked in supermarkets but when was soup invented? The design of the soup bowl and soup spoon varies from country to country, but the earliest surviving soup bowl was excavated from Xianrendong Cave in China, which is believed to date back to 20,000 BCE, so humanity has been eating soup for a very long time indeed. Soup may have been consumed even earlier than this by Neanderthal people all over the world, as archaeologists believe that hot stones were used to boil water to cook food. Boiled bones from animals and poultry make what we would now call "stock", which is frequently used to add flavour to soups.

The word soup may be derived from the Italian word *zuppa* or the French *soup,* which in turn comes from the Latin word *suppa,* meaning bread that has been steeped in liquid. Breadcrumbs are frequently added to soup mixtures. In Germany, the word *sup* means to liquidise or turn to liquid, which is a description of soup to most people. In the Caribbean, the soup pot is permanently on the stove, a hotpot which has a flavour and to which more ingredients can be added. There are wedding soups, Christmas soups, vegetable soups and meat soups as you will discover below.

The history of soup-making began when humanity was able to cook in vessels, made of earthenware or ceramic. A ceramic statue, the Venus of Dolní Věstonice, was found in Brno in the Czech Republic and this is believed to date to 28,000 BCE.

This is regarded as the earliest example of ceramic sculpture made by humanity. Early ceramic pots and pans enabled humans to boil water, and also make soups from the bones of trapped animals. Nowadays in a commercial kitchen, making soup involves time-consuming processes like chopping, simmering, pureeing and liquidising. Over time, making soup has become a mix of tastes from leftover food, re-cooked and adding extra flavour using herbs, spices and stock from meat bones. However, the invention of the soup-maker can take a lot of that hard work from the process, allowing you to just choose the ingredients, pop them in the machine and shortly afterwards, enjoy your soup.

TYPES OF SOUPS

There are 101 recipes for you to try but before that, let's look at 12 different types of soup made worldwide so you find it easier to choose.

- *Consommé*. This is a thin, clear, honey-coloured, transparent soup, first made in France. The colour changes depending on the product used to make it, with poultry producing a lighter shade than a meat-based soup. The recipe utilizes egg whites to clear the soup and it is famous for being simmered for a long time, to remove any impurities. Using egg whites to ensure that any oil and fat will adhere to the eggs allowed all fat to be removed completely before serving. Some chefs reportedly strain off the fat using a fine mesh or cheesecloth, and after that, the soup may be refrigerated for days to ensure that all fat has been skimmed off. To serve, the soup had a dash of sherry, chopped vegetables or an egg yolk.

- *Bisque* is a French word to describe a thick soup whose basis is seafood, cooked with cream to ensure a smooth consistency. The seafood used varies from crab to crayfish, lobster or shrimp and some chefs also use the shell of the seafood, ground to a powder, added as a thickener for this soup. The important aspect is the timing of the addition of the cream because a good bisque needs to have cream added early, with other stock or liquid added gradually to reduce the cream, to ensure the final taste. This soup is served after it has been pureed and then strained carefully.

- *Broth* is a thick soup, common in Ireland and Scotland, cooked with pieces of meat and vegetables, both of which are still evident when it is served. Broth is accompanied by thick slices of bread.

- *Chowder* is a thick soup made with clams, and it was first made in the US, where three varieties exist. The difference is often the colour of the soup because each variety has slight differences. Manhattan chowder uses red clam chowder and contains tomatoes which give that colour tint to the soup, whereas New England chowder has a whiter appearance due to the cream or milk included in its ingredients and it is commonly known as "White" chowder.

Rhode Island chowder tends to have a clear, transparent appearance compared to the other two because no tomatoes or dairy products are included in the ingredients.

- *Cold soup*. Cucumber soup is an example of a cold soup, with its cool, green colour perfect for a hot summer's day and the invention of Gazpacho, the cold tomato soup, was a method of utilizing a glut of tomatoes, with added garlic and stale bread to make the delicious red soup we all love to order! Fruit soups are made in several countries and served cold in Central European landlocked cities and examples are Hungary's *Meggyleves* (literally cherry soup) or *Gyümölcs leves* (fruit soup). I tried these first on Margit Island in Budapest in a sizzlingly hot summer and it is a really refreshing taste on a hot summer's day.

- *National soups* were originally made in one country eg Mulligatawny soup or French onion soup. Most countries have at least one typical soup and international chefs enjoy sharing their national soups, making them new favourites in our kitchens.

- *Christmas soup* comes from Guyana, and this Pepperpot is the national dish. It consists of meat, (usually chicken but could be pork) cooked with rice and curry flavouring. The cooking takes place in a large pot and takes many hours. Thickening is provided by rice and not flour, unlike European traditions. In Scandinavia, *Frukstoppa*, a cold fruit soup, is also served at Christmas and during the festive season.

- *Miso soup* from Japan is made by fermenting soybeans, mixed with salt and *kōji,* which is a fungus to aid the fermentation process. Miso is widely utilized in Japanese cooking for pickling and preserving vegetables but the delicious Miso soup can be made in seconds by adding a spoonful of Miso curd to hot water, like making tea. With a soup-maker, you can use fresh beans, and Miso paste to make a wonderful, high-protein soup bursting with vitamins and minerals or simply use a teaspoon of the curd to add its wholesome and nutritious flavour to your soups.

- *Spicy* soups are very common in Asia and *Jjamppong* hails from Korea, which combines noodles with an extremely spicy seasoning. Not for the faint-hearted! Chinese cooking offers many spicy soups too and Thailand has a different mix of ingredients using lemongrass to tempt the soup lover.

- *Thickened soups* have added flour, rice or other ingredients to give them a thick, often chunky consistency and texture.

- *Vegetable soups*, use any available in the country of origin and often arrive with toppings such as grated cheese or croutons. Pea soup and bean soup are common in Germany, Japan, Mediterranean countries and worldwide. Cherokee Native Americans used three ingredients to make Three Sisters Soup, using three available vegetables; sweetcorn, beans and squash or pumpkin. Their method of cultivating these three crops together is still widely used in agriculture today.

- *Wedding soup* despite the name, was not eaten to celebrate the union of a couple on their wedding day. The name originates in a mistake made in the translation from Italian to English, of *minestra maritata,* which literally means a married soup, in the sense that the flavour is produced by mixing the meat, pasta and vegetables, making a culinary "marriage" in the kitchen. In Italy, *minestra* is simply vegetable soup whereas in some parts of the US and around the world, "Wedding soup" is still served under this name.

7 TIPS AND TRICKS

1. Don't overfill the soup maker. Make sure to leave enough room in the pot for the ingredients to expand as they cook. Overfilling the pot can cause the soup maker to malfunction or not work properly.

2. Chop your ingredients into small pieces to ensure that they cook evenly and quickly.

3. Consider using a blend of soft and hard vegetables for optimal texture. For example, soft vegetables like tomatoes and bell peppers can add flavor, while harder vegetables like carrots and potatoes add body to the soup.

4. If you want a creamier soup, try adding coconut milk or cream at the end of the cooking process.

5. Add herbs and spices at the end. If you add them at the beginning of the cooking process, they can lose their flavor. Instead, try adding them towards the end of the cooking time or after the soup has finished cooking.

6. To make a heartier soup and more thick soup, try adding grains like beans, rice, quinoa, or lentils to the mix.

7. Use a soup maker to save time. A soup maker can puree and cook soup in one pot, so you don't have to transfer it to a separate pot to cook it. This can save a lot of time, especially if you're making a bigger amount of soup.

HOW DOES A SOUP MAKER WORKS?

Soup makers are usually cylinder shaped, similar to a kettle or a blender with a heating function to cook the ingredients. Various buttons control whether your finished soup is chunky or smooth or completely clear. They also offer a cook the advantage of cooking the soup in just one kitchen appliance, helping to save both time and effort and allowing for easy clean-up of just one appliance, not several pots and pans.

Traditionally, soup is made slowly starting with chopping ingredients, and then simmering them in liquid or stock, to cook slowly to soften the ingredients. After this, the chef sieves, strains or uses a food processor to achieve a smooth consistency. In the past, some soups were a treat, for invalids or a delicacy and took a very long time to make, which was a joy for a chef. However, for people with busy lives, a soup maker can cut hours off that preparation time and also save a lot of time cleaning up afterwards because the only thing to clean is your soup maker. Usually electric, a soup maker can produce your soup in about 25-30 minutes and it offers a range of functions such as blending ingredients for a smooth consistency or sautéing them if you require it.

Next section gives you 101 recipes to choose from. Your soup maker allows you to decide how many people will be eating it and adjust quantities. At the switch of a button, you can choose a smooth, chunky, or medium texture for your soup. Push a button to pre-cut the veg or to sauté for a while, before adding extra liquid or stock. Let your soup-maker do all the hard work while you work, do the shopping, collect children from school, enjoy a cup of tea in the garden or do some other task. Another advantage of a soup maker is that it saves space in your kitchen. Instead of using lots of pots frying and then a saucepan, you can just pop everything into your soup maker, press a button, and your soup arrives in less than 30 minutes. With only one utensil to clean, this also saves time afterwards too. Its compact design is useful and you can also use it to puree food for babies and even to make smoothies.

Ready to start? Let's look at some famous, national soups to whet your appetite.

National soups to try using your soup-maker.

1. China: Chicken and sweetcorn soup is a favourite in Chinese restaurants.
2. France: French Onion soup topped with cheese and croutons.
3. Germany: *Griessknödel* soup, has dumplings added, made of semolina.
4. Great Britain: Oxtail soup uses the tail to make a tasty soup.
5. Hungary: *Goulash* uses paprika, grown locally is a spicy, meaty soup.
6. Italy: Minestrone is famous worldwide and is also known as Wedding Soup.
7. Spain: *Gazpacho* is a cold tomato soup, with added breadcrumbs and garlic.
8. Sweden: *Fruktsoppa* contains many different kinds of fruit, and is served cold.
9. The US: Chowder is believed to have been first made in Manhattan.
10. The Philippines: *Sinigang* has a savoury and sour taste, which is due to its ingredients, namely Tamarind which grows so well in the area.
11. Russia, Ukraine and Poland: *Borsch (or Borshch, Borsht),* or beetroot soup, makes a really colourful pink soup that is served with sour cream or natural yogurt. There is a Russian recipe and a slightly different Ukanian recipe, and it is also made in Poland.

VEGAN SOUP MAKER RECIPES

1. Seaweed Mushroom Soup

Servings| 3 Time|15minutes

Nutritional Content (per serving):

Cal | 205 Fat | 2g Protein |3.6g Carbs| 47.1g Fibre| 2.1g

Ingredients:

- 40 g (1/8 cup) margarine
- 40 g (1/8 cup) flour
- 15 ml (1 tablespoon) brandy
- 300 ml water (1 ½ cups)
- 15 cm (6 inches) of dried kombu seaweed
- 1 dried mushroom (shiitake here)
- 15 ml (1 tbsp) of tamari
- 150 to 200 ml (1/2 cup to 1 cup) hot vegetable milk

- 1 squeeze of lemon juice
- 80 g (1 ¼ cups) of or shiitake mushrooms
- 150 g (5 ounces) fresh oyster mushrooms 1 tbsp high temperature resistant oil
- 1 grain(pinch) of ground black pepper
- 1 grain (pinch) of salt

Directions:

1. In your soup maker, bring the water, the Kombu seaweed and the dried mushroom to a high heat. Once it simmers, turn off the heat and let steep for at least 15 minutes (1 hour or overnight if possible). After resting, filter your mixture and add the tamari.
2. Clean the mushrooms and cut them into strips. Turn on the sauté button in your Soup maker and add sauté the mushrooms for a few minutes in a frying pan in vegetable oil.
3. In a small saucepan, form a creamy sauce béchamel with the margarine and the flour, dilute with the brandy and the water infused with mushrooms and seaweed. Finish with the hot vegetable milk.
4. Gently squeeze some lemon juice but be careful not to add so much lemon juice. Once the béchamel has thickened, pour it into the soup maker and finish with the sautéed mushrooms on top.
5. To reheat, do not hesitate to put in the oven for a few minutes at 180°C.
6. Serve with toasted bread and a salad.

2.   CABBAGE AND RED LENTIL SOUP

Servings| 6 Time|30 minutes

Nutritional Content (per serving):

Cal | 164 Fat | 4.2g Protein |7.5g Carbs| 26g Fibre| 3g

Ingredients:

- 15 ml (1 tbsp) of olive oil
- 1 leek
- 1 stalk of celery
- 4 leaves of green cabbage (or kale)
- 6 carrots
- 1 head of broccoli

- 1 litre of water
- 150 g (1 ½ cups) red lentils
- ½ tbsp curry powder
- 220 ml coconut milk
- 1 grain (pinch) of salt
- 1 grain (pinch) of ground black pepper

Directions:

1. Wash and cut the vegetables into small pieces.
2. Turn on the sauté button in your soup maker and sauté the leek and celery in olive oil for a few minutes. Then add the carrots, broccoli and green cabbage.
3. Then add the water and bring it to a boil for about 5 minutes
4. Rinse the red lentils and add them to the soup
5. Then, add the curry and cook for about 25 minutes maximum.
6. At the end of cooking add the coconut milk, salt and pepper and stir.
7. Ladle your soup in serving bowls
8. Serve and enjoy your soup!

3. SPLIT PEA SOUP

Servings| 3 Time|30 minutes

Nutritional Content (per serving):

Cal | 250 Fat | 2g Protein |15g   Carbs| 30g Fibre| 2.5g

Ingredients:

- ❖ 3 green leeks
- ❖ 100 g (1 cup) split peas
- ❖ 2 white (or orange) carrots
- ❖ 1 celery stalk
- ❖ 2 grams (1 pinch) of nutmeg

- ❖ 1 pinch of turmeric
- ❖ some seeds
- ❖ 120 millilitres (1/2 cup) of vegan cream
- ❖ 1 grain (1 pinch) of salt
- ❖ 1 grain (1 pinch) of ground black pepper

Directions:

1. About 4 hours before making the soup, soak the split peas in water.
2. Wash the leek greens and slice them very finely.
3. Wash the carrots and cut them into chunks.
4. Rinse the split peas and drain it very well
5. Put all the vegetables in your soup maker and cover with boiling water
6. Add the celery stalk and let simmer with the cover on for 30 minutes.
7. Once the timer is up, turn off your soup maker
8. Remove the celery stalk and blend the soup.
9. Add the turmeric, nutmeg, salt, and pepper.
10. Ladle your soup in serving bowls; then serve with vegetable cream and sprinkle with seeds.
11. Enjoy your soup!

4.   CARROT SOUP

Servings| 4 Time|30 minutes

Nutritional Content (per serving):

Cal | 105 Fat | 2.3g Protein |3g Carbs| 19g Fibre| 2 g

Ingredients:

- ❖ 1 kg (2 pounds) of carrots
- ❖ 5 grams (1 tbsp) of frozen chopped garlic
- ❖ 4 grams (1 tsp) of ground cumin

- ❖ 2 vegetable stock cubes
- ❖ 30 millilitres (2tbsp) of soy cream
- ❖ 1 grain (1 pinch) of ground black pepper

Directions:

1. Cut the carrots into cubes after washing and cleaning it
2. Pour the water in your soup maker; and add in the stock cube
3. Add in the garlic, the cumin and the ground black pepper to taste.
4. Cover your soup maker and cook for 20 minutes
5. If the carrots aren't tender, you can cook again for 10 additional minutes
6. Add the soy cream
7. Mix everything, and then ladle your soup in serving bowls
8. Serve and enjoy your soup!

5. CHESTNUT SOUP

Servings| 3 Time|15 minutes

Nutritional Content (per serving):

Cal | 280 Fat | 10g Protein |3g Carbs| 36g Fibre| 2.7g

Ingredients:

- ❖ 1 onion
- ❖ 30 millilitres (1 tbsp) of oil (preferably olive)
- ❖ 500grams (1 pound) cooked chestnuts
- ❖ 500 millilitres (2 cups) of vegetable stock

- ❖ 250 millilitre (1 cup) of soy cream
- ❖ 500 millilitres (2 cups) of water
- ❖ 1 grain (1 pinch) of salt
- ❖ 1 grain (1 pinch) of ground black pepper

Directions:

1. Peel the onion and cut it into thin strips.
2. In your soup maker, turn on the function sauté, and sauté the onion in olive oil.
3. When the onions begin to turn translucent, add the chestnuts, then the broth and the soy cream.
4. Season with salt and pepper to taste.
5. Lock the lid and set the time for 15 minutes (a little longer if you are using raw chestnuts).
6. Once the time is up mix everything to obtain a nice velvety texture. You can add a little water (or soy milk) if the soup seems too thick.
7. Serve hot, without delay.

6.   SQUASH SOUP

Servings| 5 Time|25minutes
Nutritional Content (per serving):

Cal | 183 Fat | 10g Protein |2.3g Carbs| 13.2g Fibre| 2.9g

Ingredients:

- 1 kg butternut squash (2 pounds)
- 1 large potato
- 75 grams of red or yellow lentils
- 1 turnip (1/4 cup)
- 1 large carrot (optional)

- 15 millilitres (1 tbsp) of oil (olive if possible)
- 1 litre (4 cups) of water
- 30 millilitres (2 tbsp) of soy sauce
- 1 grain (1 pinch) of salt
- 250 millilitres (1 cup) of vegetable cream (optional)

Directions:

1. Start by preparing your vegetables; peel and cut the potatoes, squash, turnip and carrot into large cubes (you can also choose to put the turnip and carrot in their skins if they are young).
2. Peel the onion and cut it into large cubes. In your soup maker; turn on the function sauté; then heat in the oil for about 5 minutes, stirring occasionally. Add the soy sauce and mix, leaving on the heat for a few seconds to sauté the onion.
3. Pour in the water, the cubed potatoes, turnips, carrots, squash and lentils.
4. Lock the lid and cook for 20 minutes; then mix and season with the salt
5. Your soup should be very creamy and soft. When ready to serve, add a little vegan cream to each bowl if desired.

7.   RADISH SOUP

Servings| 4 Time|30 minutes

Nutritional Content (per serving):

Cal | 99.9 Fat | 2g Protein |2.9g   Carbs| 19.3g Fibre| 3.2g

Ingredients:

- ❖ 1 large onion
- ❖ 2 large potatoes
- ❖ 1 turnip (optional)
- ❖ 500 grams (1 pound) of radishes with nice tops

- ❖ 15 millilitre (1 tbsp) of vegetable oil (olive if possible)
- ❖ 1 litre of water
- ❖ 30 millilitres (2 tbsp) of soy sauce (optional)
- ❖ 1 grain (1 pinch) of salt
- ❖ 250 millilitres (1 cup) of Vegetable cream (optional)

Directions:

1. Prepare the vegetables: peel and cut the potatoes and the turnip into large cubes (you can also choose to put the turnip with its skin if it is young).
2. Separate from the radishes (you will eat them separately) the tops and wash them carefully several times, removing the yellowed tops if necessary.
3. Peel the onion and cut it into large cubes. In your soup maker, press the function sauté; and heat the oil over a medium heat for about 5 minutes, then add the onions and sauté while stirring occasionally.
4. Add the soy sauce and mix very well and sauté for 2 minutes; then pour in the water, the cubed potatoes, turnips, and radish tops.
5. Cover the soup cooker, and cook for about 20 minutes, the vegetables must be well cooked).
6. Mix, and add salt if necessary.
7. When ready to serve, add a little vegetable cream to each bowl if desired.
8. Serve and enjoy your soup!

8.   TOMATO SOUP

Servings| 4-5 Time|25 minutes

Nutritional Content (per serving):

Cal | 147.9 Fat | 6.6g Protein |4g Carbs| 22.6g Fibre| 2.3g

Ingredients:

- ❖ 500g peeled and seeded tomatoes
- ❖ 2 garlic cloves, finely minced
- ❖ 1 small onion
- ❖ 15 millilitres (1 tbsp) of olive oil

- ❖ 15 grams (2 tbsp) of whole sugar
- ❖ 500 millilitres (2 cups) of vegetable broth
- ❖ Herbs of your choice (oregano, basil, etc.)
- ❖ 1 grain (1 pinch) of salt
- ❖ 1 grain (1 pinch) of ground black pepper

Directions:

1. Peel and seed the tomatoes. Cut the flesh into pieces.
2. In your soup maker, sauté the peeled and chopped garlic and onion for 5 minutes after pressing the button "sauté.
3. When your ingredients become translucent, add the tomato pieces, sugar and herbs and season very well
4. Sauté everything for about 5 minutes; pour in your vegetable broth. Lock your soup maker with the lid and let simmer for 20-25 minutes
5. Ladle your soup in serving bowls; then serve and enjoy your soup!

9.   SPLIT PEA AND CARROT SOUP

Servings| 3 Time|30 minutes

Nutritional Content (per serving):

Cal | 94.3Fat | 1g Protein |5.9g   Carbs| 17.8g Fibre| 6.5g

Ingredients:

- ❖ 45 millilitres of vegetable oil (3 tbsp)
- ❖ 1 large, chopped onion
- ❖ 2 celery stalks chopped
- ❖ 2 chopped carrots (1 cup)
- ❖ 1 litre (4 cups) of vegetable broth
- ❖ 500 grams (1 pound) of rinsed yellow split peas
- ❖ 3 bay leaves
- ❖ 1 grain (1 pinch) salt
- ❖ 1 grain (1 pinch) of ground black pepper to taste

Directions:

1. Turn on the function sauté of your Soup maker and sauté the onions, the carrots and the celery in the oil for 10 minutes, while stirring occasionally.
2. Add the vegetable broth, drained peas, and the bay leaves.
3. Bring to a boil; then cover and cook for 25 minutes
4. Season with salt and pepper to taste
5. Serve and enjoy your soup!

10.   BROCCOLI SOUP

Servings| 6 Time|25 minutes

Nutritional Content (per serving):

Cal | 334Fat | 12g Protein |12g   Carbs| 39g Fibre| 4g

Ingredients:

- ❖ 30 ml olive oil (2 tbsp)
- ❖ 1 onion, coarsely chopped
- ❖ 1 kg of broccoli (flowers) (2 pounds)
- ❖ 500 ml almond milk (2 cups)
- ❖ 1 litre (4 cups) of vegetable broth
- ❖ 500 grams (2 pounds) of rinsed yellow split peas
- ❖ 3 bay leaves
- ❖ 1 grain (1 pinch) of salt
- ❖ 1 grain (1 pinch) of ground black pepper to taste

Directions:

1. In your soup maker, turn on the function sauté, heat the olive oil and add the onion, sauté for a few minutes.
2. Add the broccoli florets, vegetable broth and almond milk, season and lock the soup maker with the lid
3. Let simmer until the broccoli is cooked, for about 15 minutes.
4. Remove the mixture from your soup maker to a blender and blend until smooth.
5. Season; and top with toasted slivered almonds, and finish with chopped chives.
6. Serve and enjoy your soup!

11. VERMICELLI SOUP

Servings| 3-4 Time|35 minutes

Nutritional Content (per serving):

Cal | 135 Fat | 4g Protein |3g Carbs| 18g Fibre| 2g

Ingredients:

- ❖ 250 grams of split peas (1/2 pound)
- ❖ 2 medium onions
- ❖ 1 carrot
- ❖ 1 liter (4 cups) of water

- ❖ 2.8 grams of cumin (1 pinch)
- ❖ 1 bay leaf
- ❖ a handful of vermicelli
- ❖ ½ lemon
- ❖ 30 grams (2 tbsp) of chopped parsley

Directions:

1. Start by rinsing the split peas and draining them, thinly slice or chop the onions, cut the carrots into small cubes.
2. Heat the oil in your soup maker by pressing the button function "sauté" and add the onions, sauté until translucent, add the split peas, pepper, cumin and bay leaf
3. Add in the water after turning off the button sauté and press the button "smooth" because the split peas absorb a lot and the soup may be too thick. Close the soup maker and cook for about 30 minutes.
4. Remove the bay leaf, mix the soup; add the salt the handful of vermicelli and let cook for additional 10 minutes by pressing the button "chunky"
5. At the end of cooking add the lemon juice and sprinkle with chopped parsley.
6. Serve immediately, sprinkling with cumin and a few drops of lemon if desired.
7. Serve and enjoy your soup!

12.   LEEK SOUP

Servings| 4 Time|30 minutes
Nutritional Content (per serving):
Cal | 165 Fat | 3.5g Protein |5g   Carbs| 12g Fibre| 3g

Ingredients:

- 500 grams (1 pound) of yellow split peas
- 100 grams (1/2 cup) of yellow lentils
- 30 millilitres of olive oil (1 tbsp)
- 1 large, sweet onion, chopped
- 1 white leek, chopped
- 1 handful of dried pumpkin seeds
- 1 grain of salt (1 pinch)

- 3 garlic cloves, crushed (1 tbsp)
- 2 large carrots cut into cubes
- 2 sprigs thyme, plus a few leaves for garnish
- 1 litre (4 cups) of vegetable broth
- 1 handful sunflower seeds
- 1 grain (1 pinch) of ground black pepper

Directions:

1. Prepare all your vegetables.
2. In your soup maker, put the split peas and pour over the litre and a half of boiling water over it, press the function button "smooth" and cook at a low boil for 15 minutes, the peas should be a little tender but not cooked.
3. Remove the split peas and drain it very well when the timer is off
4. At the same time, roast the seeds in a pan without fat
5. Clean the soup maker and turn on the sauté function button; then heat the olive oil over in it.
6. Add the onion, the leek, the garlic, the carrot and the thyme and let melt for about 5 minutes, the onion should be very translucent and tender.
7. Add the split peat to the vegetables with the broth and 3 cups of water.
8. Press the button function "smooth" and cook for about 20 minutes
9. Remove the thyme then mix with an immersion blender.
10. Adjust the seasoning; the, serve with the seeds and a few thyme leaves as decoration
11. Enjoy your soup!

13.   YELLOW CARROT SOUP

Servings| 4 Time|35 minutes

Nutritional Content (per serving):

Cal | 125Fat | 3.1g Protein |3.3g   Carbs| 17g Fibre| 2.6g

Ingredients:

- ❖ 250 grams of Leek (the white part) (1/2 pound)
- ❖ 250 grams o of sweet Potato (1/2 pound)
- ❖ 250 grams (½ pound) of White or yellow carrots
- ❖ 1 bunch of Celery
- ❖ 1 large white onion
- ❖ 1 cube of Vegetable or poultry broth
- ❖ 1 litre (4 cups) of water
- ❖ 1 garlic clove
- ❖ 15 millilitres (1 tbsp) of Olive oil

Directions:

1. Peel the carrots and the potato and cut into cubes. Wash the leek and the white celery and cut it into strips - chop the onion and the garlic clove.
2. Press the button sauté in your Soup maker and sauté the onion, the garlic and the leek for about 5 minutes; add the rest of the ingredients - cover with the water and season with the salt and the ground black pepper and let simmer for about 30 minutes, after pressing the button "smooth"
3. Ladle the soup in serving bowls
4. Serve and enjoy your soup!

14.   CABBAGE AND CELERY SOUP

Servings| 3-4 Time|30 minutes

Nutritional Content (per serving):

Cal | 95Fat |2g Protein 3g   Carbs| 12g Fibre| 1.8g

Ingredients:

- ❖ 1 white head of cabbage
- ❖ 1 white onion
- ❖ 1 garlic clove
- ❖ 1 vegetable broth cube
- ❖ 1 bunch of celery, about 250 grams (1/2 pound)

- ❖ 1 grain (1 pinch) of fresh coriander
- ❖ 1 teaspoon paprika
- ❖ One teaspoon of ginger
- ❖ One teaspoon of turmeric

Directions:

1. Remove the first leaves from the cabbage, roughly mince and rinse well in cold water.
2. Peel; then slice the onion and the garlic. Cut the white celery into small pieces.
3. Put everything in your Soup maker with the vegetable cube, the grated ginger, a little chopped cilantro; then cover with water and press the button function "smooth" and cook for 35 minutes. At the end of cooking, turn off the soup maker
4. Serve and enjoy your soup!

15.   ARTICHOKE SOUP

Servings| 4 Time|15 minutes

Nutritional Content (per serving):

Cal | 223Fat | 6g Protein |5g   Carbs| 16g Fibre| 2.5g

Ingredients:

- ❖ 500 grams (1 pound) of artichoke
- ❖ 1 yellow onion
- ❖ 1 litres of water
- ❖ 1 grain (1 pinch) of salt
- ❖ 1 grain (1 pinch) of nutmeg

- ❖ 1 garlic clove
- ❖ 15 millilitres (1 tbsp) of olive oil
- ❖ 100 millilitres of vegan firm cream (1/4 cup)
- ❖ 1 grain of ground black pepper (1 pinch)

Directions:

1. Carefully peel and wash the artichoke pieces, slice them and finely chop the onion.
2. Add the vegetables into the broth; then pour everything in your soup cooker and cook pressing the button "smooth" for about 15 minutes
3. Season with the salt and the ground black pepper
4. When you are ready to serve, reheat the stew if necessary, then serve in small bowls, adding the heavy vegan cream to each and sprinkling with a touch of grated nutmeg.
5. Serve and enjoy your soup!

16.   BEET SOUP

Servings| 3-4 Time|20 minutes

Nutritional Content (per serving):

Cal | 198Fat | 5g Protein |6g Carbs| 14.5g Fibre| 1.6g

Ingredients:

- 500 grams (1 pound) of cooked beets
- 2 and a half-peeled tomatoes,
- the juice of 1/2 a lemon
- 30 millilitres (2 tbsp) of olive oil

- 1 litre (4 cups) of water,
- 1 and a half cube of vegetable stock,
- 1 large onion
- 60 grams of vegan cream (1/4 cup)

Directions:

1. Start by peeling and chopping the onion.
2. Cut the beets and tomatoes into regular pieces.
3. In a heated soup maker, put the beets, the tomatoes, the onion, the water and the vegetable broth.
4. Cook for about 20 minutes using the button function "smooth".
5. When the timer is off; add the lemon juice and the vegan cream.
6. Add the salt and the ground pepper.
7. Taste and adjust the seasoning if necessary.
8. Ladle your soup in serving bowls
9. Serve and enjoy your soup!

17.   SPINACH SOUP

Servings| 4   Time|20 minutes

Nutritional Content (per serving):

Cal | 140Fat | 3g Protein |5g   Carbs| 17g Fibre| 3g

Ingredients:

- ❖ 30ml of olive oil (2 tbsp)
- ❖ 1 onion, minced
- ❖ 15 grams of finely chopped parsley (1 tbsp)
- ❖ 500 grams (1 pound) of watercress
- ❖ 250 grams (1/2 pound) of spinach
- ❖ 1 litre of vegetable stock (4 cups)
- ❖ 500 g potatoes (1 pound), cut into small cubes

Directions:

1. Heat the olive oil in your soup maker by pressing the button "sauté"
2. Add the onion, the parsley, the watercress, the spinach, and sauté for five minutes.
3. Add the vegetable broth, the potatoes, and season.
4. Close the soup maker for 20 minutes.
5. Ladle your soup in serving bowls
6. Serve and enjoy your soup!

18.   ASPARAGUS SOUP

Servings| 3-4   Time|25 minutes

Nutritional Content (per serving):

Cal | 215Fat | 5.9g Protein |5g   Carbs| 15.6g Fibre| 2.3g

Ingredients:

- 500 g (2 cups) of asparagus
- 250 millilitres (1 cup) of cashew nut cream
- 1 half onion
- 30 grams of chopped parsley (1 tbsp)
- 250 millilitres (1 cup) of vegetable broth
- 1 grain (1 pinch) of salt
- 1 grain (1 pinch) of white pepper

Directions:

1. Start by cleaning the asparagus.
2. In your soup maker; press the sauté button and add in the broth, place the asparagus and cover.
3. Turn off the button sauté and press the button smooth instead
4. Cook for about 25 minutes; then remove the asparagus.
5. Slice the half onions and sauté them in the sauté pan.
6. Remove the caramelized onions from the skillet.
7. In the bowl of a blender, put the asparagus, the half onions, the cashew nut cream, the salt, the pepper, the chives and the vegetable broth mixture
8. Blend to obtain a smooth cream.
9. Immediately pour into each bowl and sprinkle with finely chopped parsley
10. Serve and enjoy your soup!

19. CELERY SOUP

Servings| 3Time|30minutes

Nutritional Content (per serving):

Cal | 136Fat | 2g Protein |2.36g Carbs| 13g Fibre| 2g

Ingredients:

- ❖ 30 millilitres (2 tbsp) of vegetable oil
- ❖ 1 medium onion
- ❖ 1 medium head of celery
- ❖ 250 millilitres (1 cup) of vegetable stock
- ❖ 1 grain (1 pinch) of salt
- ❖ 1 grain (1 pinch) of pepper

Directions:

1. Chop the celery and the onion
2. Heat the oil into your soup maker by pressing the button "sauté" then pour in the stock
3. Let your ingredients simmer for about 25 minutes, by pressing the function button smooth
4. Once your soup is ready; let it cool for about 5 minutes; then puree it with an immersion blender if it is not smooth enough
5. Pour the soup into serving bowls; then top it with parsley
6. Serve and enjoy your soup!

20.   BROCCOLI SOUP

Servings| 3Time|30minutes

Nutritional Content (per serving):

Cal | 250 Fat | 3g Protein |3.2g Carbs| 14g Fibre| 2g

Ingredients:

- ❖ 500 grams (1 pound) of chopped broccoli
- ❖ 1 grain (1 pinch) of ground black pepper
- ❖ 4 grams of garlic powder (1 tbsp)

- ❖ 250 millilitres of vegetable stock (1 cup)
- ❖ 1 grain (1 pinch) of salt

Directions:

1. In your soup maker, combine all together the chicken broth with the broccoli, the salt, the ground black pepper, and the garlic powder.
2. Close the lid of the soup maker and cook for about 15 minutes, or until the broccoli is soft.
3. If your soup is not smooth; puree for a few seconds
4. Pour your soup into two separate serving bowls
5. Serve and enjoy your soup!

VEGETARIAN SOUP RECIPES

21. GREEN BEAN SOUP

Servings| 4Time|25minutes

Nutritional Content (per serving):

Cal | 235 Fat | 10g Protein |7g   Carbs| 13g Fibre| 3g

Ingredients:

- ❖ 500 g of green beans (2 cups)
- ❖ 1 onion
- ❖ ½ litre of chicken broth (2 cups)
- ❖ 50 grams of fresh cream (1/4 cup)

- ❖ 50 grams of chives (2 ½ tbsp)
- ❖ 1 grain (1 pinch) of salt
- ❖ 1 grain (1 pinch) of ground black pepper
- ❖ 30 millilitres of vegetable oil (2 tbsp)
- ❖ 30 grams of butter (2 tbsp)

Directions:

1. Start by stalking then washing the green beans.
2. Peel and chop the onion.
3. Heat olive oil and 1 knob of butter in your soup maker by pressing the button "sauté".
4. Sauté the chopped onion for a few minutes.
5. Add the green beans and stir for a few minutes.
6. Pour the chicken broth.
7. Add the chives but keep a few sprigs for decoration.
8. Cover and cook for 25 minutes using the button "function smooth".
9. Once the beans are cooked but still slightly crunchy.
10. Season with the salt and the ground black pepper.
11. Add the fresh cream over the top.
12. Ladle your soup in serving bowls.
13. Serve and enjoy your soup!

22. ZUCCHINI SOUP

Servings| 3Time|20minutes

Nutritional Content (per serving):

Cal | 123 Fat | 4g Protein |3.6g   Carbs| 16.6g Fibre| 2g

Ingredients:

- 3 medium peeled and chopped yellow onions
- 1 washed and chopped zucchini
- 10 chopped leaves of kale
- 1 chopped head of broccoli
- 1 litre of vegetable broth (4 cups)
- 1 minced head of garlic

- 30 grams of packed cilantro (2tbsp)
- 30 grams of packed parsley (2 tbsp)
- Juice of 1 lemon
- 30 millilitres of unrefined olive oil
- 1 grain of sea salt (1 pinch)

Directions:

1. In your soup maker, press the button "sauté"; place the oil and let heat
2. Add the onions and cook it for about 5 minutes; stir from time to time
3. Add the zucchini, the kale and the broccoli; then let cook for about 5 additional minutes.
4. Pour in the vegetable stock and turn off the function "sauté" and press rather the function "smooth" and cook for about 20 minutes
5. Turn off the heat and add the garlic, then let it cool for about 15 minutes
6. Season with the salt and sprinkle the parsley and cilantro over the top
7. Serve and enjoy your soup!

23. BRUSSELS SPROUT SOUP

Servings| 4Time|25minutes

Nutritional Content (per serving):

Cal | 177 Fat | 11g Protein |6g Carbs| 4.5g Fibre| 3.2g

Ingredients:

- ❖ 30 millilitres of olive oil (2 tbsp)
- ❖ ¼ chopped onions
- ❖ ½ chopped stalk of celery
- ❖ 1 large peeled and sliced carrot
- ❖ ½ small green cabbage head chopped into pieces
- ❖ 2 minced garlic cloves
- ❖ 500 millilitres (2 cups) of beef stock or broth

- ❖ 50 grams of fresh chopped parsley (1/4 cup)
- ❖ 5 grams of dried thyme (1 pinch)
- ❖ 5 grams of dried rosemary (1 pinch)
- ❖ 5 grams of garlic powder (1 pinch)
- ❖ 1 grain of salt (1 pinch)
    1 grain of freshly ground black pepper

Directions:

1. Heat the oil in your soup maker over a medium heat, by pressing the button function "sauté"
2. Add in the onions and cook for about 3 to 4 minutes
3. Add in the celery and the carrots to the pan and mix through the different flavours
4. Cook for about 3 to 4 minutes; then add in the cabbage and cook for 5 additional minutes
5. Add in the stock, the parsley and the herbs, the onion or garlic powder and let simmer on a medium low heat, then turn off the button "sauté" and press the button "smooth"
6. Cover with a lid and let simmer for about 10 to 15 minutes
7. Season with the of salt and the ground black pepper
8. Add in a little bit of extra herbs
9. Serve and enjoy your soup warm!

24. ASPARAGUS AND ZUCCHINI SOUP

Servings| 4Time|25minutes

Nutritional Content (per serving):

Cal | 177 Fat | 11g Protein |6g   Carbs| 4.5g Fibre| 3.2g

Ingredients:

- ❖ 750 grams of asparagus (1 ½ pounds)
- ❖ 1 medium zucchini
- ❖ 1 or 2 celery sticks
- ❖ 1 medium onion
- ❖ 30 grams of tahina (2 tbsp)

- ❖ 2 peeled garlic cloves
- ❖ ½ grated, peeled lemon
- ❖ 1 grain of black pepper (1 pinch)
- ❖ ½ litre of water (2 cups)
- ❖ 30 millilitres (2 tbsp) of olive oil

Directions:

1. Preheat your oven to a temperature of about 200°C (400°F).
2. Cut the asparagus into pieces of about 5 cm (2 inches) each.
3. Slice your zucchini into round slices.
4. Cut the celery into pieces and slice the onion into pieces too.
5. Add the garlic and the vegetables to a heat proof tray.
6. Drizzle the vegetables with a little bit of olive oil; then roast it in the oven for about 20 minutes.
7. Remove your vegetables from the oven and transfer it to your soup maker with the grated lemon peel.
8. Add the water and press the button function "Smooth" and cook for about 25 minutes.
9. Season your soup with salt and pepper.
10. Drizzle the tahini over your soup; then serve and enjoy your soup with a salad!

25. AVOCADO SOUP

Servings| 3 Time|15 minutes

Nutritional Content (per serving):

Cal | 109 Fat | 9g Protein |5g Carbs| 7g Fibre| 3g

Ingredients:

- 6 trimmed and chopped spring onions
- 2 peeled garlic cloves
- 2 halved ripe avocados
- 15 millilitres of lime juice (1 tbsp)
- 1 grain (¼ Tsp) of freshly ground cumin
- 500 millilitres (1 pound) of vegetable stock
- 250 millilitres (1 cup) of almond milk
- 1 additional chopped avocado; coriander leaves for garnish!

Directions:

1. Put all the ingredients into your soup maker and add in the stock.
2. Press the button function "smooth".
3. Cook for about 10 to 15 minutes.
4. Remove the soup from the heat and serve it into bowl.
5. Serve and enjoy your soup with tomato slices and avocado!

26. NETTLE SOUP

Servings| 3 Time|15 minutes

Nutritional Content (per serving):

Cal | 249 Fat | 14g Protein |10g   Carbs| 23g Fibre| 2.6g

Ingredients:

- ❖ 30 millilitres (2 tbsp) of olive oil
- ❖ 250 grams (1/2 pound) potato , diced
- ❖ 750 millilitres (3 cups) of vegetable broth
- ❖ 500 grams of nettles (1 pound)
- ❖ 150 millilitres of cooking soy (1/2 cup)

Directions:

1. Start by heating the olive oil in your soup maker by pressing the button function "sauté". Add in the diced potatoes and turn off the button "sauté" then add in the vegetable broth and press the button "smooth"
2. Cook for about 15 minutes.
3. Meanwhile, wash the nettles and dry them very well. Keep only the thinnest leaves and stems. Add them to the pan with the potatoes and continue cooking for 5 minutes.
4. Add in the cooking soya; then serve hot.
5. Enjoy your soup!

27. WHITE BEAN SOUP

Servings| 4 Time|25 minutes

Nutritional Content (per serving):

Cal | 230 Fat | 29g Protein |17g   Carbs| 26g Fibre| 2.3g

Ingredients:

- 30 millilitres (2 tbsp) of olive oil
- 1 large, chopped onion
- 2 finely minced garlic cloves
- 1 finely chopped large carrot
- 1 chopped celery rib
- 1 litre (4 cups) of vegetable broth
- 5 grams of dried thyme (1 pinch)
- 3 grams of oregano (1 pinch)
- 1 grain of kosher salt (1 pinch)
- ½ grain of black pepper (1/2 pinch)
- 250 grams of white drained and rinsed beans
- 150 grams of baby spinach
- Fresh chopped parsley
- 100 grams of grated parmesan cheese for serving

Directions:

1. In your soup maker and after pressing the button "sauté"; heat the olive oil; then add in the onions and sauté for about 3 to 5 minutes
2. Add in the garlic, the carrots, the celery, the thyme, the oregano, the salt and the pepper and cook for about 2 to 3 minutes
3. Add the vegetable broth and the beans; then turn off the button function "sauté" and press the button "smooth instead"
4. Cook for about 15 minutes
5. Add in the spinach and cook for about 2 additional minutes
6. Remove from the heat; then sprinkle with fresh parsley and with the grated parmesan cheese
7. Serve and enjoy your soup!

28. CASHEW SOUP

Servings| 3 Time|45 minutes

Nutritional Content (per serving):

Cal | 179 Fat | 14g Protein |11g   Carbs| 8g Fibre| 3g

Ingredients:

- ❖ olive oil as desired
- ❖ 250 grams of chopped crimini mushrooms
- ❖ 1 Chopped shallot
- ❖ 1 Minced garlic clove
- ❖ 1 litre (4 cups) of low sodium vegetable broth
- ❖ 1 grain (1 pinch) of sea salt
- ❖ 1 grain (1 pinch) of ground black pepper
- ❖ 2 grams of dried thyme
- ❖ 100 grams of cashew cream made of 150 grams of raw cashews (1/2 cup)

Directions:

1. Start by sautéing the mushrooms, the shallot and the garlic over a medium heat for about 10 minutes
2. Pour in the vegetable broth; the salt, the pepper, and the thyme; then let simmer for about 5 minutes
3. Blend the mushrooms and the soup and blend it very well
4. Soak the cashews into hot water for about 30 minutes
5. Drain the cashews and blend it with ¼ cup of the soaking water; then pulse it very well
6. Add a little bit of water and mix very well
7. Serve and enjoy your soup with the cashew cream!

29. MINESTRONE SOUP

Servings| 4 Time|55 minutes

Nutritional Content (per serving):

Cal | 266 Fat | 12g Protein |9.8g Carbs| 15g Fibre| 2.8g

Ingredients:

- ❖ 40 grams of chickpeas (1/4 cup)
- ❖ 150 grams of black beans (1/2 cup)
- ❖ 1 litre (4 cups) of water
- ❖ 1 tomato
- ❖ 1 zucchini
- ❖ 30 grams of butter (2 tbsp)
- ❖ 1 onion
- ❖ 50 grams of vermicelli (1/4 cup)
- ❖ 150 millilitres of liquid cream (1/2 cup)
- ❖ 50 grams of fresh herbs (basil or other) (2 ½ tbsp)
- ❖ 1 grain of salt (1 pinch)
- ❖ 1 grain of ground black pepper (1 pinch)
- ❖ 250 grams of flat beans (1/2 pound)

Directions:

1. Soak the chickpeas and black beans in a bowl for 12 hours.
2. Cook the chickpeas and black beans in boiling water for 1 hour in a deep saucepan, add coarse salt then continue cooking for 30 minutes.
3. Wash and cut the tomato into cubes.
4. Wash and cut the zucchini into cubes.
5. In your soup maker, press the button function "sauté"; then melt the butter for about 3 minutes
6. Turn off the function button "sauté" and add in the chopped onion and the zucchini cut into cubes. Add the tomato, the flat beans, chickpeas, and black beans, and turn off press the button "smooth"; then cook for about 20 minutes.
7. 5 minutes before the end of cooking, add the vermicelli; Pour in the cream and adjust the seasoning.
8. Serve with the cheese, the ground black pepper and the fresh herbs
9. Enjoy your soup!

30. FENNEL SOUP

Servings| 4 Time |30 minutes

Nutritional Content (per serving):

Cal | 268 Fat | 11.6g Protein |4g   Carbs| 14.3g Fibre| 2.3g

Ingredients:

- 1 fennel
- 1 leek
- 2 white onions with their stems
- 2 garlic cloves
- 1 litre of vegetable broth (4 cups)

- 50 grams of blue cheese (3 tbsp)
- 20 grams of sesame seeds (1 ½ tbsp)
- 1 grain of salt (1 pinch)
- 1 grain of ground black pepper
- 90 grams of rice semolina (3 tbsp)

Directions:

1. Wash and peel the vegetables; then finely chop the fennel.
2. Peel and crush the garlic cloves.
3. Cut the stems of the onions, thinly slice them then thinly slice the onions.
4. Slice the leek into thin strips.
5. In your soup maker, pour the broth, and add the vegetables.
6. Press the button "smooth" and cook for about 25 minutes
7. Rinse the rice semolina under cold water and drain it very well.
8. About 3 minutes before the end of cooking, pour in the rice semolina. Adjust the seasoning.
9. Pour the soup in small bowls, crumble the cheese, and sprinkle the sesame seeds.
10. Serve and enjoy immediately your soup!

31. ORANGE SOUP

Servings| 3-4 Time|35 minutes

Nutritional Content (per serving):

Cal | 233 Fat | 12g Protein |5g Carbs| 12g Fibre| 3g

Ingredients:

- ❖ 30 grams of vegan butter (2 tbsp)
- ❖ 1 peeled and diced butternut squash
- ❖ 1 sweet peeled and diced potato
- ❖ 1 carrot, peeled, sliced
- ❖ 1 stalk of celery, chopped
- ❖ 1 sweet onion, chopped

- ❖ 2 garlic cloves, chopped
- ❖ 1 litre (4 cups) of chicken broth
- ❖ 3 small, sweet peppers, chopped
- ❖ 1 grain (1 pinch) of salt
- ❖ 1 grain (1 pinch) of ground black pepper, to taste

Directions:

1. Press the button "sauté" in your soup maker and melt the vegan butter over a medium-high heat; sauté the diced squash and sweet potato, carrot, celery, onion and garlic for 15 minutes.
2. Add the chicken broth and sweet peppers; turn off the button "sauté" and press the button "smooth".
3. Cook for about 30 minutes; then season with salt and pepper.
4. Ladle the soup in serving bowls.
5. Serve and enjoy your soup!

32. CUCUMBER AND ZUCCHINI SOUP

Servings| 3 Time|25 minutes

Nutritional Content (per serving):

Cal | 187 Fat | 6g Protein |5.3g   Carbs| 12g Fibre| 3g

Ingredients:

- ❖ 2 large English cucumbers
- ❖ 2 small carrots
- ❖ 1 zucchini
- ❖ 1 large onion
- ❖ 1 litre of vegetable broth (4 cups)
- ❖ 35 grams of butter (2 ½ tbsp)

- ❖ 1 shallot, chopped
- ❖ 50 grams of all-purpose flour (1/4 cup)
- ❖ 750 millilitres of milk (3 cups)
- ❖ 1 grain of salt (1 pinch)
- ❖ 1 grain of ground black pepper (1 pinch)
- ❖ Parsley for sprinkling

Directions:

1. Peel and thinly slice the cucumbers, carrots and zucchini. Chop the onion.
2. Add the vegetables to your soup maker; then cover and cook for 20 minutes
3. Heat the butter and shallots in a large separate saucepan, add the flour and mix very well.
4. Add the milk and cook, stirring constantly, until a creamy sauce forms.
5. Add the cucumbers; whisk well to remove lumps. Add your mixture to your Soup maker. Taste and season with salt, pepper and parsley, to taste
6. Serve and enjoy your soup!

33. BEET AND POTATO SOUP

Servings| 4 Time|70 minutes

Nutritional Content (per serving):

Cal | 203 Fat | 11.3g Protein |10g   Carbs| 11.3g Fibre| 2g

Ingredients:

* 250 grams of peeled and diced potatoes (1/2 pound)
* 250 grams of peeled and diced beets (1/2 pound)
* 15 millilitres of olive oil (1 tbsp)
* 1 grain of salt (1 pinch)
* 1 grain of ground black pepper to taste (1 pinch)
* 1 stalk of celery, chopped
* 1 onion, diced

* 1 garlic clove, minced
* 1 litre of chicken broth (4 cups)
* 3 grams of dried thyme (1 tsp)
* 1 bay leaf
* ½ litre of milk (2 cups)
* 30 millilitres of 1f lemon juice (2 tbsp)

Directions:

1. Preheat the oven to 190 ° C (375 ° F). Place the potato and beetroot cubes on a baking sheet. Brush with 1 table of olive oil; then season with salt and pepper. Bake until everything becomes tender, for about 1 hour; let cool.
2. Heat about the olive oil in your Soup Maker by pressing the button "sauté" and sauté the onion, celery, and garlic; cook, stirring, until onion is translucent, about 5 minutes.
3. Turn off the button "sauté" and press the button function "smooth".
4. Add the potato and beetroot cubes, chicken broth, thyme, and bay leaf; cook for about 45 minutes, until the celery is tender.
5. Remove the bay leaf; then remove the bay leaf.
6. Add the milk and the lemon juice, heat through.
7. Serve and enjoy your soup!

34. CARROT AND ORANGE SOUP

Servings| 3 Time|30 minutes

Nutritional Content (per serving):

Cal | 215 Fat | 10.5g Protein |5g   Carbs| 10g Fibre| 3g

Ingredients:

- 15 millilitres of rapeseed oil (1 tbsp)
- 2 finely chopped small onions
- 500 grams of carrots (1 pound)
- 2 oranges, squeezed into juice
- 1 litre of vegetable broth (4 cups)
- 65 millilitres of heavy cream
- 1 grain of salt (1 pinch)
- 1 grain of ground black pepper (1 pinch)

Directions:

1. Prepare the vegetables and roughly chop them.
2. In your soup maker, press the button "sauté" and sauté the onion in the oil for about 3 to 4 minutes
3. Add in the carrots, the orange juice; then coarsely grate the ginger and the broth; then turn off the button "sauté' and press the button "smooth"
4. Cook for about 25 minutes; then return the soup to your soup maker, add the cream and heat for a few more minutes.
5. Season with salt and pepper
6. Serve and enjoy your soup

35. CAULIFLOWER AND RADISH SOUP

Servings| 4-5 Time|25 minutes

Nutritional Content (per serving):

Cal | 225 Fat | 8.3g Protein |11g   Carbs| 15g Fibre| 1.8g

Ingredients:

- ❖ 500 grams of cauliflower (1 pound)
- ❖ 250 grams of radishes (1 cup)
- ❖ 750 millilitres of vegetable broth (3 cups)

- ❖ 1 grain of salt
- ❖ 1 grain of pepper
- ❖ 30 grams of fresh chives (2 tbsp)
- ❖ 85 millilitres of 15% cream (1/4 cup)

Directions:

1. Prepare the cauliflower; cut into large florets and boil 10 min, which corresponds to three-quarters cooking. The cauliflower will then be firmer that al dente.
2. Drain the cauliflower and place it into your Soup maker with the radish after cutting the radish into small pieces.
3. Add in the hot broth (just enough to cover the cauliflower); then press the button "smooth" and cook for about 8to10 min until the cauliflower is tender. Add salt and pepper to taste.
4. If your soup is not tender enough, puree it in a blender or food processor until it becomes smooth. Pour into a container, cover, and refrigerate for at least 2 hours before serving.
5. When ready to serve, add the cream, check the seasoning
6. Add the chopped chives. Serve and enjoy your soup

36. POTATO CHOWDER

Servings| 4-5 Time|25 minutes

Nutritional Content (per serving):

Cal | 198 Fat | 7.5g Protein |7.3g Carbs| 13g Fibre| 2.3 g

Ingredients:

- 3 chopped celery stalks
- 2 finely chopped medium onions
- 3 chopped medium leeks (the white portion only)
- 1 medium chopped green pepper
- 6 finely minced garlic cloves
- 30 millilitres of olive oil (2 tbsp)
- 4 medium peeled and cubed potatoes (1 pound)
- 750 millilitres of vegetable broth (3 cups)
- ½ grain of ground black pepper (1 pinch)
- 1 grain of salt (1 pinch)
- ¼ litre of milk, optional (1 cup)
- 2 chopped green onions

Directions:

1. In your soup maker, press the button "sauté" and sauté the celery with the onions, the leeks, the green pepper and the garlic into the oil until it becomes tender.
2. Add in the potatoes, and turn off the button "sauté"; then add in the broth, the pepper and the salt and press the button "smooth"; then reduce the heat; cover and cook for about 10 to 15 minutes; stir from time to time
3. Let your soup cool; then sprinkle with the green onions
4. Serve and enjoy your soup!

37. FENNEL AND BEAN SOUP

Servings| 4 Time|25 minutes

Nutritional Content (per serving):

Cal | 158 Fat | 3.6g Protein |8g Carbs| 23g Fibre| 2.3g

Ingredients:

- ❖ 1 large; finely chopped onion,
- ❖ 1 small; thinly sliced fennel bulb
- ❖ 15 millilitres of olive oil (1 tbsp)

- ❖ 1 litre (4 cups) of reduced-sodium chicken broth or of vegetable broth
- ❖ 250 grams of rinsed and drained cannellini beans (1/2 pound)

Directions:

1. In your soup maker, press the button function "sauté" and sauté the onion and the fennel into the oil until it becomes tender.
2. Turn off the button "sauté" and press the button "smooth"; then add in the broth, the beans, the tomatoes, the thyme, the pepper, and the bay leaf
3. Cook for about 30 minutes
4. Discard the bay leaf; then add in the spinach; then cook for about 3 to 4 additional minutes or until the spinach is wilted.
5. Serve and enjoy your soup!

38. BLACK BEAN AND LENTIL SOUP

Servings| 3 Time|30 minutes

Nutritional Content (per serving):

Cal |185 Fat | 6g Protein |10g   Carbs| 21g Fibre| 2g

Ingredients:

- 250 grams of rinsed and drained black beans (1/2 pound)
- ½ litre (2 cups) of vegetable broth
- 2 carrots
- 100 millilitres of water (1/4 cup)
- 3 grams of ground cumin
- 30 grams of chopped fresh cilantro
- 100 grams of yellow lentils

Directions:

1. Place the black beans, the lentils, the broth and the carrots, with the water and the ground cumin s well as lentil in your soup maker.
2. Press the button "smooth" and cook for about 30 minutes.
3. Unplug your soup make and ladle your soup in serving bowls.

39. CORN SOUP

Servings| 3 Time|20 minutes

Nutritional Content (per serving):

Cal | 165Fat | 4g Protein |4g   Carbs| 15g Fibre| 2g

Ingredients:

- ❖ 30 millilitres olive oil (2 tbsp)
- ❖ 2 bay leaves
- ❖ 1/2 onion, minced
- ❖ 2 clove garlic, minced
- ❖ 3 grams of ginger (1 pinch)
- ❖ 3 grams of turmeric (1 pinch)
- ❖ 750 millilitres vegetable stock (3 cups)
- ❖ 250 grams of corn (1/2 pound)
- ❖ 90 grams of fresh coriander, chopped (3 tbsp)

Directions:

1. Heat the olive oil in your soup maker after pressing the button "sauté"
2. Add in the bay leaves, the onion, garlic, ginger and turmeric, and sauté for about 5 minutes.
3. Add corn kernels, vegetable broth; season and turn off the button "sauté" and cook for 10 to 15 minutes after pressing the button "smooth".
4. Mix everything together keeping a few grains of corn for topping your soup
5. Serve and enjoy your soup with cilantro!

40. ARTICHOKE SOUP

Servings| 4Time|30 minutes

Nutritional Content (per serving):

Cal | 187Fat | 5g Protein |4g   Carbs| 16g Fibre| 3g

Ingredients:

- ❖ 750 grams of artichoke (1 ½ pounds)
- ❖ 1/2 onion
- ❖ 1/2 clove of garlic
- ❖ 500 grams of potatoes (1 pound)
- ❖ 1 litre (4 cups) of vegetable stock
- ❖ 3 grams (1 pinch) of nutmeg
- ❖ 50 grams of hazelnuts (1/4 cup)
- ❖ 30milliliters of olive oil (2 tbsp)

Directions:

1. Peel the artichokes and the potatoes, wash them, and cut them into large dice. Peel and mince the onion.
2. Heat the olive oil in your soup maker; sauté the chopped onion with the garlic.
3. Add the artichokes and potatoes, season with salt and pepper, cover with the broth and cook for 30 minutes after pressing the button "smooth".
4. Meanwhile, toast the hazelnuts in a non-stick skillet over a medium heat.
5. Blend the artichokes, add the nutmeg and sprinkle with the hazelnuts.
6. Serve and enjoy your soup!

MEAT SOUPS

41. BEEF AND VEGTABLES SOUP

Servings| 4   Time|60 minutes

Nutritional Content (per serving):

Cal | 320Fat | 12g Protein |15g   Carbs| 16g Fibre| 3g

Ingredients:

- ❖ 500 grams of beef (1 pound)
- ❖ 3 medium tomatoes
- ❖ 1 large carrot
- ❖ 3 large potatoes
- ❖ 100 grams leek (4 oz)
- ❖ 100 grams turnip (4 oz)
- ❖ 1 medium-sized onion
- ❖ 1 to 2 stalks of celery
- ❖ 1 litre of water (4 cups)
- ❖ 1 grain of salt (1 pinch)

Directions:

1. Wash and cut your meat into large pieces.
2. Start by braising your meat to tenderize it: put a large pot of water (1/2 L) on the heat (medium). Add your meat to it. Simmer, once, for 1 hour. Then, when all or most of the water has evaporated, add 1/2 L and simmer a second time for 1 hour.
3. While the meat cooks, wash and peel all your vegetables. Then cut them into medium sized pieces.
4. When the meat is almost tender, transfer it to your soup maker and add your tomatoes, potatoes, and carrots first. Then cover with 1/2 L of water.
5. Press the button "smooth" and cook for around 45 minutes.
6. Add the turnips and cook for 10 minutes.
7. At this stage, the water has evaporated a lot. Then add 1/2 litre of water. Then add the celery, onion and leek and don't forget to salt your soup. Bake for 20 minutes and it's ready.
8. Serve and enjoy your soup!

42. CHICKEN AND POTATO SOUP

Servings| 4   Time|60 minutes

Nutritional Content (per serving):

Cal | 285Fat | 11g Protein |13g   Carbs| 14g Fibre| 2.3g

Ingredients:

- ❖ 1 chicken breast, 500 grams (1 pound)
- ❖ 2 large potatoes
- ❖ 2 stalks of celery
- ❖ 1/2 onion

- ❖ 30 millilitres (1 tbsp) of olive oil
- ❖ 3 laughing cow cheese portions (or other brand of cheese)
- ❖ 1 grain of black pepper (1 pinch)
- ❖ 1 grain of salt (1 pinch)
- ❖ 1 litre of water (4 cups)

Directions:

1. Peel the potatoes, clean them and chop them coarsely. Do the same with the onion
2. Wash well and cut the celery into large pieces.
3. In your soup maker, add the chicken, and the onion with a little oil,
4. Press the button "sauté"; then add the rest of your ingredients, except for the cheese
5. Cover with water and turn off the button "sauté" and cook well over medium heat after pressing the button "smooth"
6. Cook for about 30 minutes; then remove a few pieces to garnish the soup with.
7. Mix the rest of the chicken with the other ingredients, add the pieces of cheese, and mix again.
8. Ladle your soup in a soup maker
9. Serve and enjoy your soup!

43. CHICKEN AND EGG SOUP

Servings| 4   Time|15 minutes

Nutritional Content (per serving):

Cal | 275Fat | 10g Protein |8.2g   Carbs| 13g Fibre| 2g

Ingredients:

- ❖ 1 litre of chicken stock (4 cups)
- ❖ 500 grams of thinly sliced chicken breasts (1 pound)
- ❖ 500 grams of creamed corn (1 pound)
- ❖ 4 lightly beaten eggs

Directions:

1. Pour the chicken stock in your soup maker
2. Add in the chicken and sauté for 5 minutes after pressing the button function "sauté'
3. Add in the creamed corn.
4. Turn off the button "sauté" and press the button "smooth" and cook for about 10 minutes; then whisk in the eggs.
5. Keep stirring for about 3 minutes
6. Season with the sea salt and a dash of pepper
7. Serve and enjoy your soup with bread or toast!

44. MEXICAN SOUP

Servings| 3   Time|15 minutes

Nutritional Content (per serving):

Cal | 285Fat | 11g Protein |10.5g   Carbs| 15g Fibre| 1g

Ingredients:

- ❖ 30 millilitres of olive oil (2 tbsp)
- ❖ 500 grams of boneless skinless chicken thighs, cut into pieces of about ¾ inch each (1 pound)
- ❖ 5 grams of reduced-sodium taco seasoning (1 pinch)

- ❖ 100 grams of chickpeas (1/2 cup)
- ❖ 200 millilitres of salsa (1 cup)
- ❖ 1 litre of chicken stock (4 cups)

Directions:

1. In your soup maker, press the button "sauté" and heat the oil over a medium-high heat; then add in the chicken; cook and stir for about 6 to 8 minutes.
2. Stir in the taco seasoning.
3. Add the remaining ingredients; then turn off the button "sauté" and cook for 10 minute
4. Ladle the soup in serving bowls
5. Serve and enjoy your soup!

45. CHICKEN AND ASPRAGUS SOUP

Servings| 3   Time|15 minutes

Nutritional Content (per serving):

Cal | 215Fat | 13g Protein |11g   Carbs| 13g Fibre| 2.3g

Ingredients:

- 30 millilitres of olive oil (2 tbsp)
- 100 grams of cut fresh asparagus (4 oz)
- 1 small, finely chopped onion
- 2 tablespoons of all-purpose flour
- 1 grain of salt
- 3 grams of garlic powder (1 pinch)
- 1 grain of ground black pepper (1 pinch)
- 500 millilitres of chicken broth (2 cups)
- 150 millilitres of fat-free half-and-half (1/2 cup)
- 250 grams of cubed cooked chicken breast (1/2 pound)
- 50 grams of frozen corn (1/4 cup)

Directions:

1. In your soup maker, press the button "sauté" and heat the oil; then add in the asparagus and the onion; cook and stir for about 3 to 4 minutes.
2. Stir in the flour, the salt, the garlic powder, and the pepper until it becomes blended.
3. Gradually stir in the broth and the half-and-half; then turn off the button "sauté" and press the function "smooth".
4. Cook and stir for about 10 minutes; then add in the chicken and the corn constantly.
5. Add in the chicken and the corn; then heat through.
6. Ladle in serving bowls.
7. Serve and enjoy your soup!

46. PORK AND NOODLE SOUP

Servings| 2-4   Time|15 minutes

Nutritional Content (per serving):

Cal | 116Fat | 5g Protein |8g   Carbs| 11g Fibre| 1.6g

Ingredients:

- 100 grams of chopped celery (1/2 cup)
- 50 grams of chopped onion (1/4 cup)
- 15 millilitres of olive oil (1 tbsp)
- 5 grams of minced garlic
- 1 litre of water (4 cups)
- 150 grams of cut fresh asparagus pieces (1/2 cup)
- 75 grams of chopped cabbage
- 50 grams of minced fresh parsley (1/4 cup)
- 5 grams of dried tarragon (1 pinch)
- 1 grain of cayenne pepper, optional (1 pinch)
- 2 packages 150 grams each of pork ramen noodles
- 150 grams of cubed cooked pork

Directions:

1. In your soup maker, press the button "sauté" and add the celery and the onion into the oil and sauté until it becomes tender.
2. Add in the garlic; and cook for about 1 minute; then stir in the water, the asparagus, the cabbage, the parsley, tarragon, and the cayenne; then turn off the button "sauté" and press the button "smooth" and cook for about 10 minutes
3. Coarsely crush your noodles; then add in the noodles with the packet's contents of the seasoning to your pan. Cook for about 5 minutes
4. Ladle the soup into serving bowls
5. Serve and enjoy your soup!

47. ASIAN-STYLE SOUP

Servings|4   Time|15 minutes

Nutritional Content (per serving):

Cal | 283Fat | 8g Protein |14.8g   Carbs| 13g Fibre| 2g

Ingredients:

- ❖ 15 millilitres of olive oil (1 tbsp)
- ❖ 750 grams of lean ground beef (1 ½ pounds)
- ❖ 3 minced garlic cloves garlic
- ❖ 7 millilitres of stevia drops (1/2 tbsp)
- ❖ 2 grams of fresh minced ginger (pinch)
- ❖ 2 grams of crushed red pepper (1 pinch, ¼ tsp)
- ❖ 1 bunch of sliced green onions (1/2 pound, 1 ½ cups)
- ❖ ¼ litre of beef stock

Directions:

1. Start by heating your soup maker over a medium heat
2. Add the beef meat and sauté it over a medium heat for about 5 minutes
3. Add the stevia, the ginger and the red pepper
4. Add the beef stock; and turn off the button "sauté"; then press the button function "smooth" and cook for about 15 minutes
5. Serve and enjoy the soup with cauliflower rice and top with green onions
6. Enjoy your soup!

48. BEEF AND SQUASH SOUP

Servings|3 Time|35 minutes

Nutritional Content (per serving):

Cal | 283Fat | 8g Protein |14.8g Carbs| 13g Fibre| 2.6g

Ingredients:

- ❖ 1 kilogram of peeled and diced butternut Squash (2 pounds)
- ❖ 60 millilitres of avocado oil (2 ½ tbsp)
- ❖ 1 large, chopped onion
- ❖ 1 kilogram of grass-fed beef steak (2 pounds)
- ❖ 1 litre of beef stock (4 cups)

- ❖ 2 smashed garlic cloves
- ❖ Fresh sprig of thyme
- ❖ 1 sprig of fresh rosemary
- ❖ 1 grain of salt (1 pinch)
- ❖ 1 grain of ground black pepper (1 pinch)

Directions:

1. Start by preparing the squash and peel it; then remove the seeds and dice into small cubes.
2. Pour the avocado oil in your soup maker; and press the button "sauté"
3. Add in the onion and sauté it for about 2 to 3 minutes
4. Pour in the beef stock, the herbs, the salt and the pepper
5. Turn off the button function "sauté" and press the function button "smooth"
6. Cook your ingredients; then cook for about 30 minutes
7. Top your soup with parsley
8. Remove the soup from the heat; then check if the meat has become tender
9. Serve and enjoy your soup!

49. BEEF AND ONION SOUP

Servings|3 Time|35 minutes

Nutritional Content (per serving):

Cal | 266 Fat |9g Protein |13g Carbs| 12g Fibre| 1.3g

Ingredients:

- ❖ 5 medium, thinly sliced onions
- ❖ 250 grams of beef steak (1/2 pound)
- ❖ 30 millilitres of avocado oil (2 tbsp)
- ❖ 3 sprigs of fresh thyme

- ❖ 1 grain of ground black pepper (1 pinch)
- ❖ 1 litre of beef broth (4 cups)
- ❖ 30 grams of tomato paste (2 tbsp)

Directions:

1. In your soup maker and over a medium heat; pour in the oil; then add the onion and the thyme and sauté after pressing the button "sauté" of your soup maker
2. Cut the beef meat into small cubes; then add it to the pan
3. Turn off the button sauté and press the button "smooth" instead and cook for about 15 minutes; then add in ½ litre of beef broth
4. Continue cooking for about 40 minutes; make sure to keep stirring from time to time
5. Add your tomato paste to the soup maker then add the remaining quantity of the stock
6. Let your soup cook for several additional minutes
7. Turn off your soup maker and garnish with finely sliced parsley leaves
8. Serve and enjoy your soup!

50. BEEF AND SNAP PEAS SOUP

Servings|4 Time|15 minutes

Nutritional Content (per serving):

Cal | 299Fat |13g Protein |13.5g   Carbs| 11.3g Fibre| 1.3g

Ingredients:

- 500 grams of ground beef (1 pound)
- 1 packet of frozen mixed vegetables
- 1 chicken stock cube
- ½ litre of water (2 cups)
- 1 can of tomato sauce (400 millilitres) (2 cups)
- 2 stalks of celery, chopped
- 100 grams of snap peas (1/2 cup)
- 1 onion, chopped

Directions:

1. First brown the minced meat in your soup maker, by pressing the button "sauté"
2. Then add the stock cube, water, the snap peas, the tomato sauce, celery, onion and the packet of vegetables to the soup maker, mix everything together.
3. Then launch the cooking process by pressing the button "smooth" instead of –the "sauté" function button and cook for about 15 minutes
4. Add in the minced meat and give a stir
5. Ladle your soup in serving bowls
6. Serve and enjoy your soup!

51. CHICKEN RICE SOUP

Servings|4 Time|25 minutes

Nutritional Content (per serving):

Cal | 252Fat |8g Protein |6g   Carbs| 16g Fibre| 3g

Ingredients:

- 30 millilitres (2 tbsp of extra virgin olive oil
- 200 grams (2 cups) chopped carrots
- 50 grams (½ cup of finely chopped celery)
- 50 grams of finely chopped green onions (½ cup)
- 2 finely chopped garlic cloves
- 1 litre of low-sodium chicken broth (4 Cups)
- 2 bay leaves

- ❖ 100 grams of rice (1 ½ cups)
- ❖ 1 grain of salt (1 pinch)
- ❖ 1 grain of pepper (1 pinch)
- ❖ 750 grams of cooked boneless and shredded chicken breast pieces (1 ½ pounds)
- ❖ 50 millilitres (½ cup of freshly squeezed lemon juice)
- ❖ 2 large eggs
- ❖ Freshly finely chopped parsley for garnishing

Directions:

1. In your soup maker, press the button "sauté" and heat about a small quantity of olive oil; then add in the carrots, the celery and the green onions and toss to sauté very well
2. Add in the garlic; then pour in the chicken broth and the bay leaves and turn off the function button "sauté" and press the function button "smooth"
3. Once the liquid starts boiling; add in the carrots, the celery and the green onions and toss very well together
4. Add in the chicken broth and the bay leaves; the add in the rice, the salt and the pepper
5. Cook for about 20 minutes
6. Stir in the cooked chicken; then prepare the egg lemon sauce; and to do that; whisk all together the lemon juice and the eggs; then add 2 ladles of broth from the soup maker
7. Add in the sauce to the soup and stir; then remove from the heat
8. Ladle the soup in serving bowls
9. Garnish with finely chopped fresh parsley; then serve and enjoy your soup with bread!

52. ORZO SOUP

Servings|3Time|30 minutes

Nutritional Content (per serving):

Cal | 225Fat |8.6g Protein |12g   Carbs| 15g Fibre| 2.3g

Ingredients:

- One bunch of chopped fresh parsley leaves
- 30 millilitres of olive oil
- 500 grams of boneless, skinless chicken thighs, chopped into chunks (1 Pound)
- 1 grain of Kosher salt and 1 grain (1 pinch)
- 1 grain of freshly ground black pepper (1 pinch)
- 3 minced garlic cloves
- 1 diced onion

- 3 peeled and diced carrots
- 2 diced stalks celery
- 3 grams (½ teaspoon) of dried thyme
- 1,5 litre of chicken stock (5 cups)
- 1 to 2 bay leaves
- 150 grams of uncooked orzo pasta (¾ cup)
- 1 sprig of rosemary
- The juice of 1 lemon

Directions:

1. Heat half the quantity of the olive oil in your soup maker
2. Season the chicken thighs with 1 pinch of salt and 1 pinch of pepper, to taste. Add in the chicken to the pot and press the button "sauté"; sauté for about 2 to 3 minutes; then set it aside
3. Add in the remaining quantity of oil to your soup maker; then add in the garlic, the onion, the carrots and the celery and cook while stirring for about 3 to 4 minutes
4. Stir in the thyme for about 1 minute
5. Whisk in the chicken stock; the bay leaves and about 1 cup of water; then bring to a boil
6. Add in the rosemary and the chicken stock; the bay leaves and about 1 cup of water by pressing the button "smooth"
7. Add in the orzo, the rosemary, and the chicken; then let simmer for about 10 minutes
8. Stir in the lemon juice and the parsley and season with 1 pinch of salt and 1 pinch of pepper
9. Ladle the soup into serving bowls; then serve and enjoy!

53. BEEF AND BROCCOLI SOUP

Servings|3Time|20 minutes

Nutritional Content (per serving):

Cal | 227Fat |11g Protein |11g   Carbs| 17g Fibre| 2.2g

Ingredients:

- 125 grams of finely sliced carrots (1 and ½ cups)
- 1 small or medium head of broccoli
- 30 millilitres of olive oil (2 tbsp)
- 30 grams of minced garlic (2 tbsp)
- 50 grams of finely chopped yellow onion (½ cup)
- 1 litre (4 cups) of hot water with about 2 chicken bouillons or you can simply use 1 litre (4 cups) of chicken stock

- 300 grams of grass-fed beef, chopped steak (¾ pound)
- 1 can of 400 millilitres heavy cream (14 oz)
- 2 grams (¼ tsp) of nutmeg
- 10 grams (2 tsp) of salt
- 5 grams (1 tsp) of ground black pepper
- 30 grams (2 tbsp) of all purpose or almond flour

Directions:

1. Start by cutting the broccoli into small-sized florets; then put it into a saucepan filled with hot water
2. Cook the cauliflower and the broccoli into the boiling water for about 15 minutes; then strain it and set it aside
3. Put about half the quantity of the olive oil in your soup maker and press the button sauté
4. Add in the sliced garlic and the onions into the soup maker; then mix and cook for about 2 to 3 minutes
5. Add the cauliflower and the broccoli and stir very well; then cook for about 5 minutes
6. Pour in the hot water with the chicken cubes of bouillons
7. Add the heavy cream and the chicken cuts; then mix the ingredients very well together
8. Toss in the carrots and cook your soup for about 20 minutes, making sure to press the button "smooth"
9. Serve and enjoy your soup!

54. BEEF AND MUSHROOM SOUP

Servings|4Time|35 minutes

Nutritional Content (per serving):

Cal | 235Fat |12g Protein |14g   Carbs| 18g Fibre| 3g

Ingredients:

- 1 grain of pepper (1 pinch)
- 500 grams of cut lean beef steak (1 pound)
- 30 millilitres of olive oil (2 tbsp)
- 1 chopped large onion
- 150 grams cremini mushrooms (1/4 pound)
- 30 grams (2 tbsp) of tomato paste
- 3 minced garlic cloves
- 1 litre of beef broth
- 200 grams of peeled and sliced carrots (2 cups)
- 200 grams of diced sweet potatoes (2 cups)
- 30 grams of chopped celery (¾ cup)
- 1 to 2 bay leaves
- 3 grams of thyme (½ tbs)
- 3 grams of oregano (½ tbs)
- 3 grams of dried parsley (½ tbs)
- 250 millilitres (1 cup of cold water)
- Minced, fresh parsley leaves
- 1 grain of salt (1 pinch)

Directions:

1. Put the steak pieces into a medium bowl, and season with a bit of salt and ground black pepper
2. Set the steak aside and let it marinate for about 10 minutes
3. Start your soup maker and press the button "sauté"; then add a little bit of oil and sauté the onion and the mushrooms for about 10 minutes
4. After about 12 minutes, remove the vegetables from the heat and set it aside
5. Add the prepared beef meat and sauté it in the same pan for about 8 minutes
6. Add the garlic and the tomato paste; then stir for around 30 seconds
7. Stir in the wine; then cook for 2 additional minutes
8. Add the onions and the mushrooms; then add the broth, the chopped carrots, the celery and the potatoes
9. Add the thyme, the bay leaf, the oregano, and the dried parsley
10. Turn off the function "sauté" and press the button "smooth" and cook for about 30 minutes
11. Serve and enjoy your soup!

55. NOODLE, BEEF AND BOK CHOY SOUP

Servings|4 Time|30 minutes

Nutritional Content (per serving):

Cal | 245Fat |9g Protein |12g   Carbs| 18g Fibre| 3g

Ingredients:

- ½ peeled and spiralized large zucchini, peeled
- 15 grams of minced garlic (1 tbsp)
- 500 grams of lean strip steak, beef (1 pound)
- 3 grams of crushed red pepper flakes (1/2 tsp)
- 30 millilitres of olive oil (1 and ½ tablespoons)
- 250 millilitres of hot water (1 cup)
- 100 millilitres of homemade chicken broth (1 cup)

- 1 head of roughly chopped baby Bok Choy
- 100 grams of shiitake mushrooms (1 cup)
- 100 grams of chopped green onions (1 cup)
- 1 grain of salt (1 pinch)
- 1 grain of ground black pepper (1 pinch)

Directions:

1. Season the beef meat cubes with the salt, the pepper; then pat it with the olive oil.
2. Start your soup maker; then add in the of olive oil; press the button "sauté".
3. When the oil becomes hot, add the garlic and then add the beef and let cook for about 2 minutes.
4. Remove the beef from your pot; then leave it into the garlic and set it aside.
5. Put the remaining quantity of olive oil into the pan; then add the red pepper, the Choy mushrooms and stir very well for about 3 minutes.
6. Pour in the water; then add the chicken broth and turn off the button "sauté" and cook for a few minutes.
7. Add the beef, the zucchini noodles, and about half of your green onions. Cook your soup for about 10 minutes, making sure to press the button "smooth".
8. Remove the soup from the heat; then pour it into bowls.
9. Top your noodle soup with the remaining green onions; then enjoy!

56. CANNELINI BEAN AND SWEET POTATO BEEF SOUP

Servings|3-4 Time|35 minutes

Nutritional Content (per serving):

Cal | 284Fat |11g Protein |8g Carbs| 17g Fibre| 2.3g

Ingredients:

- 1 kg of cubed lean beef meat (2 pounds)
- 15 millilitres (1 tbsp) of olive oil
- 3 large, chopped sweet potatoes
- 50 grams of chopped onions (½ cup)
- 200 grams of chopped carrots (4 cups)
- 100 grams (1 cup) of chopped celery
- 200 grams of diced tomatoes (2 cups)
- 1 litre of beef broth (4 cups)

- 30 millilitres (2 tbsp) of extra virgin olive oil
- 2 leeks, white and light green parts only, cut into 1/4-inch slices
- 15 grams (1 tbsp) of chopped fresh sage
- 250 grams (1/2 pound) of cannellini beans, rinsed

Directions:

1. Press the button "sauté" and heat the oil in your soup maker for 5 minutes.
2. Add in the leeks and cook, while stirring very often, for about 3 minutes. Stir in the sage and continue cooking for about 30 seconds.
3. Stir in the broth and the water, then press the button "smooth" and cook for about 30 minutes
4. Add the beans and chicken and cook, uncovered, stirring occasionally, until everything is heated through very well for about 10 minutes.
5. Serve and enjoy your soup!

57. GROUND BEEF SOUP

Servings|4 Time|40 minutes

Nutritional Content (per serving):

Cal | 150Fat |8g Protein |4.6g   Carbs| 14g Fibre| 3g

Ingredients:

- ❖ 250 grams of ground beef (1/2 pound)
- ❖ 5 minced garlic cloves
- ❖ 30 grams of parsley (1 tbsp)
- ❖ 60 grams of basil (2 tbsp)
- ❖ 12 grams of salt (2tsp)
- ❖ 1 grain of ground black pepper (1 pinch)
- ❖ 30 grams of tapioca starch (3 tbsp)
- ❖ 1 or 2 bay leaves

Directions:

1. Start sautéing the beef meat in your soup maker, by pressing the button "sauté" and cook with a for with a drizzle of olive oil
2. Meanwhile, cut your vegetables
3. Place the sweet potatoes and the onion into your soup maker and sauté with onion
4. Add the beef, the celery, the garlic, the diced tomatoes
5. Sprinkle the basil, the salt, the pepper
6. Pour the broth into the soup maker
7. Into a measuring glass, pour 1 cup of broth; then combine it with the tapioca starch
8. Whisk your ingredients very well; then pour it over your ingredients in the soup maker
9. Cook your soup on a high heat for about 30 minutes
10. Remove the soup from the heat
11. Ladle your soup in soup bowls; then serve and enjoy it!

58. CHICKEN MAJORAM SOUP

Servings|3 Time|30 minutes

Nutritional Content (per serving):

Cal | 188Fat |7g Protein |7g Carbs| 13g Fibre| 2.2g

Ingredients:

- ❖ 30 millilitres of extra virgin olive oil, divided (2 tbsp)
- ❖ 100 grams of chopped carrot (1 1/2 cups)
- ❖ 1 large boneless and skinless chicken breast (about 8 ounces), cut into wedges
- ❖ 1 large garlic clove, finely minced
- ❖ 1 litter (4 cups) of sodium-reduced chicken broth
- ❖ 6 grams (1 tsp) of dried marjoram

- ❖ 150 grams (1 ½ cups) of baby spinach, coarsely chopped
- ❖ 1 can of about 200 grams (1 ½) of rinsed cannellini or large Nordic beans
- ❖ 30 grams (¼ cup) of grated Parmesan
- ❖ 30 grams (⅓ cup) of loosely packed fresh basil leaves
- ❖ 1 grain (pinch) of freshly ground pepper to taste

Directions:

1. Heat about 2 teaspoons of oil in your soup maker by pressing the button "sauté"
2. Add in the carrot; and chicken; then cook, while turning the chicken and stirring frequently, until the chicken begins to brown, for about 3 to 4 minutes.
3. Add in the garlic and cook, while stirring, for 1 minute. Stir in the broth and the marjoram
4. Turn off the button "sauté" and press the button "smooth" instead.
5. Cook for about 15 minutes; then with a slotted spoon transfer the pieces of chicken to a clean cutting board to let cool
6. Add in the spinach and beans to the soup maker; then cook for about 5 minutes to combine the flavours.
7. Combine the remaining 1 tablespoon of oil, the Parmesan, and the basil in a food processor
8. Process until you get a coarse paste form, adding a little quantity of water and scrape the sides if necessary
9. Cut the chicken into small pieces. Add the chicken and pesto to your soup maker. Season with pepper; then heat until hot
10. Garnish with chopped bread
11. Serve and enjoy your soup!

59. GROUND BEEF SOUP

Servings|3-4 Time|35 minutes

Nutritional Content (per serving):

Cal |250Fat |7.8g Protein |5g   Carbs| 15g Fibre| 2.6g

Ingredients:

- ❖ 1 kg (2 pounds) of veal, cut in large cubes
- ❖ 1 pound of cherry tomatoes
- ❖ 30 grams (2 tbsp) of Tomato paste
- ❖ 500 grams (1 pound) of Carrots

- ❖ 250 grams (1/2 pound) of mushrooms
- ❖ 1 finely chopped onion
- ❖ 3 garlic cloves
- ❖ 1 litre of beef broth (3.5 cups)
- ❖ 30 millilitres (1 ½ tbsp) of Olive oil
- ❖ 50 grams (2 tbsp) Chopped Parsley

Directions:

1. Brown the minced garlic and onion in your soup maker with a little olive oil by pressing the button "sauté". Add the meat and sauté for 3 minutes; then add the peeled and the sliced carrots.
2. Add the cherry tomatoes and the concentrate. Moisten with the veal broth of water (add water if the meat is not completely covered).
3. Add the parsley and season with salt and pepper
4. Add the cleaned mushrooms and cook for about 30 minutes before the end of cooking process, make sure to turn off the button "sauté" and press the button "smooth" instead
5. Ladle your soup in serving bowls
6. Sever and enjoy your soup!

60. BEEF MEATBALL SOUP

Servings|4 Time|25 minutes

Nutritional Content (per serving):

Cal |238Fat |8g Protein |7g   Carbs| 16g Fibre| 2g

Ingredients:

- ❖ 1½ litres of veal broth (5 cups)
- ❖ 2 large carrots
- ❖ 2 potatoes

- ❖ 2 turnips
- ❖ 500 g (1 pound) of frozen beef meatballs with onion
- ❖ 30 grams (1 tbsp) of tomato concentrate

Directions:

1. Peel the vegetables and cut them into pieces.
2. Place your vegetables in your soup maker and cook them in the broth mixed with tomato puree, for about 20 minutes making sure to press the button "smooth"
3. Meanwhile, cook the beef meatballs according to the preparation instructions on the package then add them to the broth.
4. Ladle your soup in serving bowls
5. Serve with a little parsley and enjoy your soup!

FESTIVAL SOUPS

61. PUMPKIN AND ALMOND CHRISTMAS SOUP

Servings|3-4 Time|60 minutes

Nutritional Content (per serving):

Cal |289Fat |11g Protein |9g Carbs| 13g Fibre| 2.3g

Ingredients:

- 1 organic pumpkin
- 1 onion
- 1 leek
- 1 clove of garlic
- 2 sprigs of thyme
- 250 millilitres (1 ½ cups) of almond milk
- 1 bay leaf

- 30 millilitres (2 tbsp) of olive oil
- 1 grain (pinch) of salt
- 2 grains (pinches) of allspice
- 50 grams (1/2 cup) of almond puree
- 1 grain (pinch) of ground pepper

Directions:

1. Wash and slice the leek into pieces.
2. Peel the onion and the garlic.
3. Rinse the pumpkin and put it on a deep baking sheet with the bay leaf, crushed garlic, onion and leek sections. Leave to cook in a preheated oven for about 45 minutes, basting regularly with a little water (as soon as it evaporates) at a temperature of 180°C (360°F)
4. 5 minutes before the end of cooking, remove the pumpkin from the oven and collect your ingredients with their juices from the baking sheet
5. Pour half of the almond milk in your soup maker and add the onion, the leek, the garlic and the cooking juices (discard the bay leaf)
6. Drizzle with oil, sprinkle with thyme, then pumpkin with the all spice and press the button "smooth"
7. Cook for about 15 minutes; then season with salt and ground black pepper
8. Divide into 4 bowls, place the pumpkin strips on top, drizzle with a few drops of olive oil and serve immediately.

62. SWEET POTATO AND COCONUT SOUP

Servings|4 Time|25 minutes

Nutritional Content (per serving):

Cal |256Fat |12g Protein |10g   Carbs| 18g Fibre| 2.1g

Ingredients:

- ❖ 4 leeks (with the green)
- ❖ 2 sweet potatoes
- ❖ 1 onion
- ❖ 2-3 carrots
- ❖ 1 litter of chicken broth (4 cups)
- ❖ 1 bay leaf
- ❖ 240 millilitres coconut cream (1 cup)
- ❖ 30 millilitres olive oil or virgin coconut oil (2 tbsp)
- ❖ a few pink peppercorns
- ❖ 1 grain coarse salt (1 pinch)
- ❖ 1 grain ground pepper (1 pinch)

Directions:

1. Peel and wash the vegetables thoroughly.
2. Dice the sweet potatoes, slice the leeks and carrots; and then chop the onion.
3. Heat the olive oil (or coconut) and brown the cut vegetables for 5 minutes in your soup after pressing the button "sauté".
4. Add the broth (without drowning the vegetables), the bay leaf and turn off the button "sauté", then press the button "smooth" and bring to a simmer. Season with salt, cover and simmer until the vegetables are tender (about 20 minutes).
5. Remove the bay leaf; mix the soup in the blender with the coconut cream and season with ground black pepper
6. If you want a thinner soup, thin it out with a little broth (if there is any left) or water.
7. Before serving, sprinkle each plate with ground pink peppercorns
8. Serve and enjoy your soup!

63. BEET AND DUMPLINGS SOUP

Servings|5-6 Time|60 minutes

Nutritional Content (per serving):

Cal |256Fat |15g Protein |16g   Carbs| 19g Fibre| 3g

Ingredients:

- 1.5 kg (3 pounds) of raw beets
- 3 bay leaves
- a few black peppercorns
- 4-5 slices of dried porcini mushrooms
- 4 garlic cloves
- 2 vegetable stock cubes
- 2 sprigs of thyme

- 1 grain (pinch) of salt
- juice of 1 lemon

For the dumplings

- 250g (1/2 pound) of ground beef
- 1 clove of garlic
- 15 millilitres (1 tbsp) olive oil
- A few sprigs of dill
- 2 grains (pinches) sumac

To serve

- 170 grams (1/2 cup) fresh cream
- 15 millilitres (1 tbsp) of lemon juice

Directions:

1. Peel and cut the beets into cubes. Put them in your soup maker and cover with cold water.
2. Add the bay leaves, peppercorns, porcini mushrooms, thyme, peeled, degermed and crushed garlic.
3. Add the stock cubes. Bring everything to a simmer making sure to press the button "smooth"
4. Cook for about 55 minutes; then let cool for about 5 additional minutes
5. Prepare the dumplings: mix together the meat, garlic, dill and sumac.
6. Form balls the size of a small walnut. Fry them in 1 tbsp. tablespoon oil 4-5 min over high heat.
7. Reheat the borscht over low heat. Adjust the seasoning with a little of salt; and add the lemon juice.
8. Serve with fresh cream beaten with a few drops of lemon.

64. PESTO NEW YEAR'S SOUP

Servings|4 Time|20 minutes

Nutritional Content (per serving):

Cal |260Fat |14g Protein |16g   Carbs| 15g Fibre| 2.6g

Ingredients:

- 1 carrot
- 1 potato
- 1 zucchini
- 100 grams green beans
- 2 tomatoes
- 1 clove of garlic
- 1 onion
- 1 stalk of celery

- 1 bunch of basil
- 80 grams (1/2cup) small soup pasta
- 50 grams (1/4 cup) parmesan
- 30 grams (2 tbsp) of corn starch
- 15 grams (1 tbsp) of sesame seeds
- 15 millilitres (1 tbsp) of olive oil
- 1 grain (1 pinch) of salt
- 1 grain (1 pinch) of ground black pepper

Directions:

1. Peel the carrot, potato and zucchini. Wash them, and then cut them into small cubes. Peel the garlic and onion, and then chop them. Finely cut the celery into brunoise. Cut the beans into pieces. Strip and chop the basil.
2. Heat the oil in your soup maker. Add the c cut vegetables. Add the diced tomatoes and 1 litre of water. Season with salt and pepper; then cover and press the button "smooth" and cook for 20 mins. Add the pasta and cook for 10 minutes over low heat. Leave to rest for 10 mins.
3. Preheat the oven to 180°C (360°F); then mix the starch and the cheese in a dish. Season with pepper, but don't season with salt. Make 8 small heaps of the mixture on the non-stick baking sheet. Sprinkle with sesame and bake for 5 minutes, until the tiles are slightly coloured.
4. Immediately take them out of the oven and place them on a cold plate. Serve the soup very hot, with the cold tiles.
5. Serve and enjoy your soup!

65. PESTO NEW YEAR'S SOUP

Servings|4 Time|20 minutes

Nutritional Content (per serving):

Cal |270Fat |15g Protein |12g   Carbs| 22g Fibre| 2.3g

Ingredients:

- ❖ 500 grams (1 pound) very green and very firm broccoli
- ❖ 100 grams (1/2 cup) of pink berries
- ❖ 2 potatoes
- ❖ 150 millilitres (1/2 cup) of liquid cream
- ❖ 1/2 onion
- ❖ 50 grams (2 ½ tbsp) butter

- ❖ 500 millilitres (2 cups) of milk
- ❖ 15 grams (1 tbsp) icing sugar
- ❖ 100 millilitres (1/2 cup) of chicken stock (with 1 stock cube)

Directions:

1. Divide the broccoli into florets, wash them and drain them (reserve one floret for decoration).
2. Peel and cut the potatoes into pieces. Chop the half onion.
3. Melt 30 g of butter in your soup maker after pressing the button 'sauté" gently fry the onion slices until transparent.
4. Add broccoli, potatoes, and broth. Add salt and pepper; turn off the button "sauté" and press the button "smooth" and cook until the vegetables are tender (for about 20 mins).
5. Mix the soup and add the milk.
6. Add the rest of the butter and the cream. Adjust the seasoning with salt and pepper.
7. Whisk the remaining cream with the sugar, and then spread it over the soup with a few sprigs of broccoli and a few pink berries on top.
8. Serve and enjoy your soup!

66. BROCCOLI AND HAZELNUT SOUP

Servings|3-4 Time|30 minutes

Nutritional Content (per serving):

Cal |235Fat |10g Protein |14g   Carbs| 10g Fibre| 2.3g

Ingredients:

- ❖ 1 head of broccoli
- ❖ 1 onion
- ❖ 1 litre (4 cups) of oat milk
- ❖ 30 millilitres (2 tbsp) of hazelnut oil

- ❖ 15 millilitres (1 tbsp) hazelnut oil
- ❖ 50 grams (1/2 cup) roasted hazelnuts
- ❖ 1 grain (1 pinch) salt
- ❖ 1 grain (1 pinch) of ground black pepper

Directions:

1. Boil the cut broccoli in water for 15 minutes
2. Press the button "sauté" in your soup maker and sauté the chopped onion with the hazelnut oil
3. Add the Oat milk; and the broccoli and turn off the button "sauté", then press the button "smooth" instead and cook for about 15 minutes
4. After 15 minutes, mix everything with the oil. Sprinkle with salt, pepper, broccoli florets and toasted hazelnuts.
5. Serve and enjoy your soup!

67. POTATO AND COFFEE SOUP

Servings|3 Time|30 minutes

Nutritional Content (per serving):

Cal |286Fat |12g Protein |13g   Carbs| 15g Fibre| 1.8g

Ingredients:

- ❖ 500 grams (1 pound) mashed potatoes
- ❖ 250 grams (½ pound) cold butter (placed in the freezer for 1 hour)
- ❖ 150 millilitres (1 ¼ cups) of whipping cream
- ❖ 250 millilitres (1 cup) skimmed milk
- ❖ 4 grains (4 pinches) of ground coffee

Directions:

1. Peel the potatoes and cut them into cubes, then cook them in salted water, starting cold.
2. As soon as the potatoes are cooked, drain them, and put them in your soup maker with the cold butter cut into cubes. Mix, adjust the seasoning with salt, pepper, add the cream and mix again.
3. Press the button "smooth" and don't forget the mixture should be a bit liquid (if necessary, add a little milk).
4. Cook for about 10 minutes; and divide it two-thirds into four cappuccino cups.
5. Heat the milk and whip it with a mini electric whisk or and Nespresso milk frothier to obtain a light foam. Pour the cream into the cups, sprinkle with ground coffee.
6. Serve and enjoy your soup!

68. THAI LEMONGRASS SOUP

Servings|3-4 Time|30 minutes

Nutritional Content (per serving):

Cal |235Fat |10g Protein |14g   Carbs| 10g Fibre| 2.3g

Ingredients:

- 1 litre chicken stock (4 cups)
- 500 grams chicken cuts (about 1 pound)
- sliced ginger
- 5 lemongrass sticks
- 1 clove of garlic
- 6 kaffir lime leaves
- 15 grams (1 tbsp) powdered sugar
- 150 millilitres (1 cup) of nuocmam sauce
- 3 squeezed limes

- 250 millilitres (1 cup) coconut milk
- 150 grams (1 ½ cups) sliced button mushrooms
- 1 bunch of cilantro
- 2 red peppers
- 1 grated carrot
- grated ginger
- 150 grams (1 cup) diced tomato
- 1 grain (1 pinch) salt

Directions:

1. Pour the chicken broth in your soup maker; add the sliced chicken cutlets, the slices of ginger, the lemongrass cut into pieces, the minced garlic, and the lemon leaves.
2. Press the button "smooth" and cook for 15 minutes.
3. Season with the salt, sugar, the nuoc-mam sauce, and lime juice.
4. Pour in the coconut milk and stir gently then add the mushrooms
5. Let cook for 5 minutes
6. Add the cilantro, sliced peppers, carrot, the ginger and diced tomato.
7. Serve and enjoy you soup immediately!

69. CROSTINI SOUP

Servings|4 Time|20 minutes

Nutritional Content (per serving):

Cal |302Fat |13g Protein |17g Carbs| 18g Fibre| 2.7g

Ingredients:

- ❖ 1 medium potato
- ❖ 200 grams arugula
- ❖ 1 clove of garlic
- ❖ 1/2 chicken stock cube
- ❖ 15 millilitres (1 tbsp) of olive oil
- ❖ 1 grain (pinch) of salt
- ❖ 1 grain (pinch) ground black pepper

- ❖ 15 grams (1 tbsp) pine nuts
- ❖ 30 millilitres (2 tbsp) of olive oil
- ❖ 8 grains (8 pinches) of oregano
- ❖ 1 grain (1 pinch) ground pepper

For the crostini

- ❖ 8 slices of bread baguette
- ❖ 250 grams (1/2 pound) mozzarella

Directions:

1. Prepare the soup. Peel the potato and cut it into thin slices. Rinse the arugula and drain it. Peel the garlic and chop it.
2. Brown the garlic with the olive oil in your soup maker, by pressing the button "sauté" Add the potato slices and mix for 1 minute, then add the arugula and stir until wilted. Pour the water and add the 1/2 stock cube.
3. Turn off the button "sauté" and press the button "smooth" instead; and cook for 15 minutes
4. Prepare the crostini. Cut the mozzarella into slices. For the larger ones, cut them so as to obtain 2 or 3 strips. Drain on several layers of paper towel. Lightly toast the baguette slices.
5. Turn on your broiler. When the soup is cooked, blend it and keep warm.
6. Spread the mozzarella over the slices of bread, sprinkle with pine nuts, salt, pepper and oregano. Drizzle with oil and slide in the oven, under the broiler. Cook for a few minutes until the mozzarella begins to melt.
7. Pour the soup into 4 bowls, season with pepper, add a drizzle of oil
8. Serve and enjoy your soup with Crostini!

70.   BARLEY SOUP

Servings|5Time|70 minutes

Nutritional Content (per serving):

Cal |350Fat |8g Protein |9g   Carbs| 13g Fibre| 2.6g

Ingredients:

- ❖ 30 millilitres (2 tbsp) of olive oil
- ❖ 200 grams pearl barley
- ❖ 4 kale leaves
- ❖ 1 bunch baby carrots or 3 carrots
- ❖ 1 leek
- ❖ ❖ 1/4 celeriac
- ❖ 1 grain (pinch) ground pepper
- ❖ 1 beef stock cube

Directions:

1. Peel and wash all the vegetables and cut them into cubes.
2. Brown all the vegetables except the cabbage in your soup maker with a drizzle of olive oil.
3. Add the cabbage in strips, the barley; the broth dissolved in a glass of hot water, salt, pepper and 1 litre of water
4. Press the button "smooth" and cook for about 35 minutes
5. Once the timer is off, check and cook for an additional 35 minutes
6. Serve and enjoy your soup!

71. FISH SOUP

Servings|4   Time|30 minutes
Nutritional Content (per serving):
Cal |320Fat |10g Protein |13g   Carbs| 15g Fibre| 2g

Ingredients:

- 1.5 kg (3 pounds) mixed small rock fish
- 500 grams (1 pound) tomatoes
- 1 large onion
- 1 white leek
- 1 small green pepper
- 4 garlic cloves
- 4 sprigs of dried fennel
- 1 sprig of dried thyme
- 2 bay leaves

- 3 stalks of parsley
- 4 grains (4 pinches) of saffron threads
- 60 millilitres (4 tbsp) of olive oil
- 1 grain (pinch) salt
- 1 grain (pinch) of ground black pepper

For the "rust"

- 3 cloves of garlic
- 2 fresh red peppers
- 100 grams (1/2 cup) of sandwich bread
- 30 millilitres (2 tbsp) of olive oil
- 4 grains (4 pinches) of saffron powder
- 1 grain (1 pinch) of coarse sea salt

To serve

- slices of toasted bread

Directions:

1. Scale the fish, gut them, rinse them, and pat them dry. Wash the tomatoes and cut them into quarters. Peel the onion; then slice it and the white leek. Peel the garlic cloves and roughly chop them. Wash the bell pepper and cut it into thin strips.
2. Heat the oil in your soup maker and press the button "sauté"; sauté the onion, garlic, leek, and pepper. Then add the tomatoes, fennel, thyme, bay leaf, parsley, saffron and fish. Add salt and pepper. Mix for 2 minutes, then cover and press the button "smooth" after turning off the button "sauté" and cook for 10 minutes. Then pour 1 litre of boiling water, cover, and cook for 20 minutes.
3. Prepare the rust: peel the garlic cloves and roughly chop them. Wash the peppers and cut them in half; remove the seeds and the stalk, coarsely chop the pulp. Put it in the bowl of a food processor with the garlic, saffron and coarse salt. Mix until you obtain a cream. Add the breadcrumbs, and then mix again. Finally, drizzle in the oil, whisking constantly, until you obtain a thick, fragrant, rust-coloured sauce
4. Pass your soup through a sieve, pressing well to extract all the juice from the fish.
5. Pour your soup in the soup maker again, filtering it and heat for a couple of minutes
6. Pour the soup into a tureen and serve at the table immediately, with the rust on the side.
7. You will spread it on the slices of toasted bread before plunging them into the soup.
8. Enjoy your soup!

72. HAKE AND POTATO SOUP

Servings|4Time|15 minutes

Nutritional Content (per serving):

Cal |312Fat |10g Protein |13g   Carbs| 16g Fibre| 2.8g

Ingredients:

- ❖ 900 grams (about 2 pounds) of hake
- ❖ 750 grams (1 ½ pounds) potatoes
- ❖ 1 large tomato
- ❖ 3 cloves of garlic
- ❖ 1 onion

- ❖ 1/2 green pepper
- ❖ juice of 1 lemon
- ❖ 1 large bunch of cilantro
- ❖ 30 millilitres (2 tbsp) of olive oil
- ❖ 1 pinch of salt

Directions:

1. Peel the garlic and the onion and cut them into very small cubes, along with the bell pepper. Grate the tomato: you recover the juice and the pulp by easily removing the skin. Peel the potatoes and cut them into 1/2 cm thick slices.
2. Put all the vegetables in your soup maker and add 1/2 l of water.
3. Press the button "smooth" and cook for about 15 minutes; the potatoes should be tender. Season with salt, add the oil and keep warm.
4. Place the fish in a steamer basket and cook for 5 minutes over a pan of simmering water. Remove from the heat, sprinkle with lemon juice and let stand for 1 minute.
5. Rinse the cilantro and chop it.
6. Remove the skin and bones from the fish and divide it among four soup bowls
7. Pour the soup over and sprinkle with cilantro
8. Serve and enjoy your soup!

73. SALMON AND POTATO SOUP

Servings|4Time|15 minutes

Nutritional Content (per serving):

Cal |312Fat |10g Protein |13g Carbs| 16g Fibre| 2.8g

Ingredients:

- ❖ 450 grams (1 pound) fresh skinless salmon
- ❖ 2 shallots
- ❖ 250 grams (1/2 pound) potatoes
- ❖ 1 lite (4 cups) of fish stock

- ❖ 50 grams (1/4 cup) of liquid cream
- ❖ 40 grams (2 tbsp) butter
- ❖ 60 grams slightly stale bread baguette
- ❖ 50 grams (3 tbsp) seaweed flakes

Directions:

1. Peel and finely chop the shallots. Peel the potatoes and cut them into large dice. Cut the salmon into large dice, removing the bones if necessary.
2. In your soup maker and after pressing the button "sauté", melt half the quantity of butter. Add the shallots and let them brown for 5 minutes.
3. Add the potatoes and the fish stock. Turn off the function button "sauté" and press the button "smooth" instead; cook covered for 15 to 20 minutes depending on the size of the potatoes. Add the salmon and continue cooking for 5 minutes.
4. With a skimmer, collect 4 pieces of salmon, reserve them.
5. Add the cream, the salt and the ground black pepper.
6. Cut the bread into small cubes.
7. Melt the rest of the butter in a skillet. Add the bread croutons and brown them, stirring regularly. At the last moment, sprinkle them with seaweed flakes.
8. Serve your soup with the seaweed croutons and the 4 pieces of crumbled salmon.

74. MISO AND ZUCCHINI SOUP

Servings|3 Time|10 minutes

Nutritional Content (per serving):

Cal |250Fat |12g Protein |11g Carbs| 13g Fibre| 2g

Ingredients:

- 6 instant miso soups
- 1 carrot
- 1 piece of ginger
- 1 clove of garlic
- 6 sprigs of cilantro

- 30 millilitres (2 tbsp) of sesame oil
- 1 zucchini
- 1 cabbage leaf
- 30 millilitres (2 tbsp) of soy sauce
- 1 litre of water

Directions:

1. Peel the carrot and the zucchini, leaving a little green, cut them into thin strips. Finely chop the cabbage leaf.
2. Peel the ginger and garlic, chop them
3. Brown all these ingredients in your soup maker with a drizzle of sesame oil, making sure to press the button "sauté" cooking for 5 minutes over low heat, then pour in the water
4. Turn off the button "sauté" and press the button "smooth" and cook for 8 minutes
5. Add the instant sachets, stir well and, as soon as it boils, remove from the heat, add the chopped coriander, a few drops of soy sauce and serve.
6. Serve and enjoy your soup!

75. CLAM AND SEAWEED SOUP

Servings|3Time|10 minutes

Nutritional Content (per serving):

Cal |298Fat |14g Protein |13g Carbs| 18g Fibre| 3g

Ingredients:

- ❖ 900 grams (2 pounds) of clams
- ❖ a piece of kombu seaweed
- ❖ 100 grams (1 cup) of turnips
- ❖ 50 grams of red miso
- ❖ Chopped chive

Directions:

1. Place the clams in salted water to drain them, refrigerate for one hour.
2. Make slits on a piece of kombu seaweed and leave to infuse for 2 hours in a bowl with 1 litre of water.
3. Cut the turnips into cubes.
4. Pour the kombu water into your soup maker with the turnips and clams.
5. Press the button "smooth" and cook for about 15 minutes; then remove the seaweed and lower the heat to reduce the broth.
6. Add 50 g of red miso with a strainer to avoid lumps.
7. Keep the soup in your soup maker warm for 3 minutes.
8. Add the chives and serve and enjoy your soup!

76. CLAM, SEAWEED AND RADISH SOUP

Servings|4 Time|20 minutes

Nutritional Content (per serving):

Cal |365Fat |10g Protein |17g   Carbs| 17.5g Fibre| 2.3g

Ingredients:

- 450 grams (1pound) of clams
- 1 grain (1 pinch) of slat
- 1 grain (1 pinch) of ground black pepper
- 3 rectangles of kombu seaweed
- 5 large, dried anchovies
- 30 grams (1/2 cups) white radish
- 1 red pepper
- 1 spring onion

Directions:

1. Sort the clams, discarding any that are broken or that don't close when tapped gently. Put the remaining ones in a large bowl with the salt and immerse them in cold water. Cover with aluminium foil, and let the clams soak in the refrigerator for 2 hours, then drain them and rinse them for a long time under cold water.
2. Put the seaweed and anchovies in a large bowl, cover them with 1 litre of boiling water and let them soak for 10 minutes; then place the seaweed and the soaking liquid in your soup maker, make sure you don't crowd your soup maker
3. Add the white radish cut into sticks, the chilli seeded and cut into thin rings and the minced spring onion. Season and press the button "smooth" then cook for about t20 minutes.
4. Remove, from the first bubbles, the seaweed and the anchovies from the liquid and throw them away. Add the clams and cook for 2 or 3 minutes, skimming off the impurities that form on the surface with a spoon.
5. The clams should now be opened. Discard any that have remained unopened and serve immediately.
6. Serve and enjoy your soup!

77. CELERIAC AND EGG SOUP

Servings|4 Time|20 minutes

Nutritional Content (per serving):

Cal |365Fat |10g Protein |17g   Carbs| 17.5g Fibre| 2.3g

Ingredients:

❖ 900 grams (2 pounds) celeriac
❖ 1 celery heart
❖ 50 grams (2 ½ tbsp) of heavy cream
❖ 4 fresh eggs
❖ 30 millilitres (2 tbsp) of white vinegar
❖ 1 grain (1 pinch) coarse salt
❖ 1 grain (1 pinch) of ground black pepper

Directions:

1. Peel the celeriac, rinse it and cut it into large cubes. Put them in your soup maker and add in 1/2 litre of water. Season with salt, and cook for about 35 minutes making sure to press the button "smooth"
2. Reserve the tender green part of the celeriac. Chop the rest and add it to the soup maker 2 minutes before the end of cooking.
3. Mix everything very well incorporating the cream.
4. Poach the eggs. Boil water high in a sauté pan with the coarse salt and white vinegar; then lower the heat. Crack the eggs separately into bowls and slide them one by one into the simmering water. Let them poach for 3 minutes: using two spoons pinch the edges of the white to seal them and coat the yolk. Drain the eggs with a slotted spoon and plunge them into cold water to stop the cooking.
5. Pour your soup into serving bowl; then place an egg on each and sprinkle with the reserved celery leaves.
6. Season and serve immediately your soup! Enjoy!

78. NOODLE AND DRIED FISH SOUP

Servings|4 Time|20 minutes

Nutritional Content (per serving):

Cal |330Fat |11g Protein |14g   Carbs| 16g Fibre| 2g

Ingredients:

- ½ litre of chicken broth (2 cups)
- 250 millilitres (1 cup) of coconut milk
- 10 grams '(2 teaspoons) of 2 tbsp curry powder
- 15 grams (1 pinch) of shrimp paste
- 1 grain (1 pinch) ginger powder
- 1 grain (1 pinch) turmeric powder

- 1 grain (1 pinch) of chilli powder
- 1 lemongrass stick
- 125 grams (1/4 pound) firm tofu
- 2 Chinese cabbage leaves
- 1 handful of bean sprouts
- 250 grams (1/2 pound) rice noodles _
- 1 hard- boiled egg
- 2 grains (2 pinches) of dried fish

Directions:

1. Heat the chicken broth in your soup maker, pressing the button function "smooth"; then add the coconut milk, the curry powder, the shrimp paste, the ground ginger, the turmeric powder, the chilli powder and 1 stick of lemongrass. Leave to cook for 5 mins.
2. Fry the 125 grams of firm tofu cut into strips. Add them to the broth with 2 shredded Chinese cabbage leaves, 1 handful of bean sprouts and 250 grams of boiled rice noodles for 2 minutes
3. Before serving, add 1 hard-boiled egg cut into quarters and 1 tbsp. tablespoons of dried fish.
4. Serve and enjoy your soup!

79. CHESTNUT AND COFFE SOUP

Servings|3 Time|10 minutes

Nutritional Content (per serving):

Cal |280Fat |10g Protein |13g Carbs| 19g Fibre| 1.2g

Ingredients:

- ❖ 250 grams of cooked chestnuts
- ❖ 1 onion browned in butter
- ❖ 250 milliliters (1 cup) of milk
- ❖ Celery
- ❖ 1 grain of instant ristretto coffee

- ❖ 150 milliliters (1 cup) of cream
- ❖ 50 grams (1 cup) of parmesan cheese
- ❖ 1 grain (1 pinch) salt
- ❖ 1 grain (1 pinch of ground black pepper)

Directions:

1. In your soup maker, poach 250 grams of cooked chestnuts with the onions browned in butter
2. Pour in the milk, a little celery, salt, and pepper.
3. Mix everything finely with a little cream, you can add water if necessary
4. Cook for about 5 minutes; by pressing the button "smooth".
5. Ladle your soup in serving cups with a little ristretto coffee and grated parmesan
6. Serve and enjoy your soup!

80. PISTACHIO TRUFFLE SOUP

Servings|4 Time|25 minutes

Nutritional Content (per serving):

Cal |233Fat |11.3g Protein |10.8g   Carbs| 10g Fibre| 0.9g

Ingredients:

- ❖ 500 grams (1 pound) of unsalted natural ground pistachios
- ❖ 1/4 bunch of celery
- ❖ 1 apple
- ❖ 500 milliliters (2 cups) of milk
- ❖ 500 milliliters (2 cups) of chicken broth
- ❖ 250 milliliters (1 cup) of liquid cream
- ❖ 3 grams (1/2 tsp) of allspice
- ❖ 1 grain (1 pinch) of ground black pepper
- ❖ 1 small jar of broken truffles
- ❖ 30 milliliters (2 tbsp) of olive oil
- ❖ 100 grams of finely chopped parsley (1/2 cup)
- ❖ 1 grain (1 pinch) of ground pepper

Directions:

1. Pour the broth and milk into your soup maker, add the ground pistachios, celery and apple cut into cubes, the allspice, the black pepper, the salt, the parsley
2. Press the button "smooth" and cook for about 25 minutes
3. Add the cream, the olive oil to your soup maker and cook for about 5 additional minutes
4. Add the rest of the whipped cream, adding the broken truffles and the parsley.
5. Add in the cream and stir
6. Divide the hot soup into 6 bowls, top them with a spoonful of whipped cream and serve immediately.
7. Enjoy your soup!

Snacks, sauces, and sides

81. SAUCE HOLLANDAISE

Servings|2 Time|15 minutes

Nutritional Content (per serving):

Cal |103Fat |5g Protein |6g Carbs| 11g Fibre| 1.3g

Ingredients:

- ❖ 170g of (about 1 cup) of butter
- ❖ 2 egg yolks

- ❖ 1 lemon
- ❖ 1 grain (1 pinch) of salt
- ❖ 1 grain (1 pinch) of ground black pepper

Directions:

1. Melt the butter in a microwave; then put it in a cup.
2. Separate the yolks from the egg whites and squeeze the lemon.
3. In your soup maker, pour the egg yolks and the lemon then mix.
4. Once the mixture has cleared up, heat up your soup maker and add the melted butter while continuing to mix.
5. Press the button smooth and cook for 3 to 5 minutes
6. Serve and enjoy!

82. SAUCE BECHAMELLE

Servings|3 Time|10 minutes
Nutritional Content (per serving):
Cal |103Fat |11g Protein |12g Carbs| 12g Fibre| 1.3g

Ingredients:

- ❖ 50 grams (1/4 cup) of butter
- ❖ 50 grams (1/4 cup) of flour
- ❖ 500 millilitres (2 cups) of milk
- ❖ 1 grain (1 pinch) of pepper
- ❖ 1 grain (1 pinch) of salt
- ❖ 1 grain (1 pinch) of nutmeg

Directions:

1. Put just a little water in the bottom of your soup maker so the milk doesn't stick. Then just add all the ingredients.
2. Press the button "smooth" and cook for about 10 minutes
3. Use or serve and enjoy your sauce!

83. SAUCE BOLOGNESE

Servings|4 Time|30 minutes

Nutritional Content (per serving):

Cal |150Fat |5g Protein |6g Carbs| 11g Fibre| 1.6g

Ingredients:

- 250 grams (1/2 pound, 1 cup) of minced beef
- 50 grams (1/4 cup) of sausage meat
- 50 grams (1/4 cup) of bacon
- 250 grams (1/2 pound) of fresh chopped tomatoes
- 1 small carrot
- a stalk of celery
- a yellow onion
- 30 milliliters (2 tablespoons) of red wine
- a clove of garlic
- 1 bay leaf
- 30 grams (1/4 cup) of basil
- 1 grain (1 pinch) salt
- 1 grain (1 pinch) of ground black pepper
- 15 grams (1 tablespoon) of tomato puree
- 1 grain (1 pinch) of thyme

Directions:

1. Peel the garlic and onion then cut them into small pieces. Do the same for the carrot. Then put all the ingredients in your soup maker, you can optionally add 90 millilitres of olive oil to spice it up a bit.
2. Press the button "smooth" and cook for about 30 minutes
3. Once the timer turns off; serve and enjoy your sauce with your favourite pasta!

84. LETTUCE AND BASIL CREAMY SAUCE

Servings|4 Time|27 minutes

Nutritional Content (per serving):

Cal |115Fat |12g Protein |7g Carbs| 12g Fibre| 2 g

Ingredients:

- ❖ 5 steamed lettuce leaves
- ❖ 200 grams (1 cup) fresh cream
- ❖ 15 milliliters (1 tablespoon) lemon juice
- ❖ 10 basil leaves
- ❖ Parsley

Directions:

1. Cut your lettuce leaves into pieces and steam them for about 20 minutes.
2. Meanwhile, heat the cream in your soup maker; and chop the basil leaves and the parsley. Once the lettuce leaves are cooked pour the cream into you soup maker; then add the lettuce leaves; the basil leaves, and the parsley and the lemon juice. And cook for about 7 minutes making sure to press the button "smooth"
3. Mix everything very finely. You should have a very light and airy texture without any lumps
4. Serve and enjoy hot with fish and vegetables

85. BERNESE SALSA

Servings|4Time|20 minutes

Nutritional Content (per serving):

Cal |115Fat |10.8g Protein |8g Carbs| 13g Fibre| 1.5 g

Ingredients:

- ❖ 3 extra-fresh egg yolks
- ❖ 120 grams (1/2 cup) butter
- ❖ 2 sprigs of tarragon
- ❖ 2 shallots

- ❖ 60 milliliters (2 tbsp) of white vinegar
- ❖ 60 milliliters (2 tbsp) of dry white wine
- ❖ 1 grain (1 pinch) of salt, ground pepper

Directions:

1. Finely chop the shallots, place them in your soup maker, and pour in the wine and vinegar. Add chopped tarragon leaves.
2. Press the button "smooth" and cook for about 20 minutes
3. Leave to cool, sieve (squeeze the shallots well to extract the gastric), add the eggs and the mi
4. Heat the butter in your soup maker after pressing the button "sauté" and add the sieved mixture, then add salt and pepper, add the rest of the tarragon leaves,
5. Serve and enjoy your salsa!

86. SWEET POTATO SAUCE

Servings|4 Time|35 minutes

Nutritional Content (per serving):

Cal |203Fat |10g Protein |4g Carbs| 15g Fibre| 1.2 g

Ingredients:

- ❖ 500 grams (1 pound) of sweet potato
- ❖ 1 onion
- ❖ 500 millilitres (1/2 litre) of stock
- ❖ 1 grain (1 pinch of spices) (curry or cumin)
- ❖ 100 millilitres of coconut cream

Directions:

1. Put the onion cut in half with 1 case of oil in your soup maker.
2. Launch the "sauté" mode (5 min) which will chop and brown the onion.
3. Meanwhile peel and chop the sweet potato.
4. Once the onion has been sautéed, add the entire remaining ingredients (cut sweet potato, broth and spices) launch the "smooth» mode (30 min).
5. Once your sauce is ready, add the coconut cream and mix. Taste to adjust seasoning with salt and pepper if needed.
6. Serve and enjoy your sweet potato sauce!

87. LENTIL DIP

Servings|4-5 Time|20 minutes

Nutritional Content (per serving):

Cal |265Fat |11g Protein |10.6g   Carbs| 13g Fibre| 1.5 g

Ingredients:

- ❖ 160 grams (1/4 pound) of coral lentils
- ❖ 250 grams (1/2 pound) peeled tomatoes
- ❖ 1 onion
- ❖ 2 cloves garlic
- ❖ 6 grams (1 tbsp) of grated ginger

- ❖ 7 grams (1 tbsp) turmeric powder
- ❖ 5 grams (1/2 tbsp) of cumin powder
- ❖ 30 grams (2 tablespoons) chopped cilantro
- ❖ 150 millilitres (1/2 cup) of water
- ❖ 90 millilitres (3 tbsp) of olive oil
- ❖ 1 grain (1 pinch) of salt
- ❖ 1 grain (1 pinch) of ground black pepper

Directions:

1. Heat the oil in your soup maker after pressing the button "sauté".
2. Peel and chop the onion and garlic.
3. Sauté the onion with the garlic and grated ginger until translucent.
4. Add your spices and lentils. Stir well then add the water and the peeled tomatoes (with their juice).
5. Cover and turn off the function "sauté" and press the button "smooth" instead and cook for 15 to 20 minutes. Adjust the seasoning if necessary.
6. Leave to cool then store in the fridge until ready to serve.
7. Serve chilled with toasted bread.
8. Enjoy your dip!

88. BEET CAPPUCCINO

Servings|3 Time|10 minutes

Nutritional Content (per serving):

Cal |110Fat |7.3g Protein |8g   Carbs| 9.1g Fibre| 2.6 g

Ingredients:

- 1 large cooked beetroot
- 1 yogurt (Activia type with lemon or other flavour)
- 250 millilitres (1 cup) fresh cream

- 15 millilitres (1 tbsp) walnut oil
- 15 millilitres (1 tbsp) balsamic vinegar
- 1 grain (1 pinch) of salt
- 1 grain (1pinch) of ground black pepper

Directions:

1. In your Soup Maker, put the cut beetroot, the yogurt, a pinch of salt and pepper, the balsamic vinegar, and the walnut oil.
2. Press the button "smooth" and cook for about 10 minutes
3. Whip the fresh cream into whipped cream.
4. Put dollops of whipped cream on the beet mixture, on top of the serving cups
5. Chill while waiting for the tasting.
6. Serve and enjoy your beet cappuccino!

89. CREAM OF CAULIFLOWER

Servings|4 Time|10 minutes

Nutritional Content (per serving):

Cal |225 Fat |10g Protein |8g Carbs| 15g Fibre| 1.8 g

Ingredients:

- 500 grams (1 pound) of cauliflower
- 250 millilitres (1 cup) of coconut milk
- 1 onion
- 1 litre (4 cups) of chicken broth

- 7 grams (1 tbsp) of curry
- 4 grams (1 tsp) turmeric
- A few sprigs of cilantro
- 1 grain (1 pinch) of salt
- 1 grain (1 pinch) of ground black pepper

Directions:

1. Wash, peel and chop the cauliflower.
2. In your soup maker, press the button "sauté" and sauté the onion with olive oil. Then add the cauliflower and sauté for a few minutes.
3. Pour the chicken broth. Season with the salt, pepper and turn off the button "sauté" and press the button "smooth" instead. Cover everything and cook for 10 minutes.
4. Add the coconut milk, curry, turmeric, and coriander.
5. In the bowl of a robot, mix everything. Pour the preparation into glasses.
6. Serve and enjoy!

90. AVOCADO MOUSSE

Servings|3 Time|8 minutes

Nutritional Content (per serving):

Cal |123Fat |10g Protein |13g   Carbs| 13g Fibre| 1.5g

Ingredients:

- ❖ 2 large avocados
- ❖ 2 lemons
- ❖ 4 nice slices of smoked salmon
- ❖ 90 millilitres (3 tbsp) heavy cream
- ❖ 2 sprigs of dill

- ❖ 1 small heart of lettuce
- ❖ 4 cherry tomatoes

For The Sour Cream:

- ❖ 30 millilitres (2 tbsp) heavy cream
- ❖ 1 squeeze of lemon juice
- ❖ 1 grain (1 pinch) of salt
- ❖ 1 grain (1 pinch) of ground black pepper

Directions:

1. Split the avocados in two. Remove the pits by pricking them with the tip of a knife. Peel off the flesh by passing a tablespoon between the pulp and the skin. Reserve the cockles.
2. Arrange the flesh of the avocados in your soup maker and sprinkle it with lemon juice. Add 2 slices of salmon, cut into strips.
3. Press the button "smooth" and cook for about 5 minutes.
4. Add to the mashed avocado, the fresh cream, a grain of salt, pepper and the sprigs of a sprig of dill. Mix and pour into the shells.
5. Cut the rest of the salmon and the lettuce into strips. Cut the cherry tomatoes into 4.
6. Spread them over the filled shells. Sprinkle with sour cream. Decorate with sprigs of dill.
7. Serve and enjoy your avocado mousse!

91. SPINACH SAUCE

Servings|3-4 Time|10 minutes

Nutritional Content (per serving):

Cal |125Fat |9.4g Protein |6.5g   Carbs| 11g Fibre| 2.3g

Ingredients:

- ❖ 250 grams (1/2 pound) of spinach
- ❖ 50 grams (1/4 cup) of flour
- ❖ 250 milliliters (1 cup) of milk
- ❖ 1 grain (1 pinch) of nutmeg

- ❖ 100 millilitres (1/4 cup) of sunflower oil
- ❖ 100 millilitres (1/4 cup) of olive oil
- ❖ A small quantity of leftover bread
- ❖ 1 grain (1 pinch) of salt
- ❖ 1 grain (1 pinch) of ground black pepper

Directions:

1. Blanch the spinach and drain it; then start your soup maker and transfer the spinach to it.
2. Add the olive oil to your soup maker and pour in the sunflower oil; add the salt, the pepper and the nutmeg.
3. Start your soup maker and press the button "sauté"; then sprinkle the spinach with the flour.
4. Pour in the milk and mix very well. Add a little quantity of butter.
5. Turn off the button "sauté" and press the button "smooth" instead and cook for about 5 minutes.
6. Cut the bread into small pieces and soak them in olive oil.
7. Sauté the bread in a skillet for a few minutes in hot oil.
8. Serve the spinach sauce in a sauce boat with the pieces of bread on top.
9. Enjoy your sauce!

DESSERT RECIPES

92.   APPLE RUHBARB

Servings|2 Time|20minutes

Nutritional Content (per serving):

Cal |200Fat |1g Protein |1.3g   Carbs| 28g Fibre| 0.5g

Ingredients:

- ❖ 4 stalks of rhubarb
- ❖ 1 golden apple

- ❖ 40 grams (1/4 cup) of brown sugar
- ❖ 6 grams (1 tbsp) of vanilla sugar (optional)
- ❖ 500 millilitres of water (2 cups)

Directions:

1. Prepare the rhubarb by peeling it and cutting it into dices. Peel and core the apple and cut it the same way.
2. Put the fruit in your soup maker. Pour in the water, then add the brown sugar and vanilla sugar (if using).
3. Press the button "smooth" and cook for about 20 minutes
4. Leave to cool before enjoying.
5. Serve and enjoy your rhubarb!

93. HAZELNUT CHOCOLATE SPREAD

Servings|6 Time|20 minutes

Nutritional Content (per serving):

Cal |275Fat |6g Protein |4g Carbs| 13g Fibre| 0.8g

Ingredients:

- ❖ 250 grams (1/2 pound) of whole hazelnuts
- ❖ 90 grams (1/2 cup) of chocolate or milk chocolate
- ❖ 150 milliliters (1/2 cup) peanut oil or hazelnut oil

- ❖ 75 grams (1/4 cup) of liquid cane sugar
- ❖ 1 grain (1pinch) of salt

Directions:

1. Start by preheating your oven to 180°C (360°F) and line a baking sheet with parchment paper.
2. Arrange the hazelnuts in a single layer, spreading them over the baking sheet. When the oven is hot, put them in the oven to roast them for 8 to 10 minutes. They must be very fragrant and slightly golden in the middle.
3. Put the roasted hazelnuts in your soup maker then press the button "smooth"
4. Break the chocolate into your soup maker; then add the oil to your hazelnuts
5. Cook for about 5 minutes; add the ground almonds and continue mixing cooking for 5 additional minutes
6. Pour the spread into a sterilized jar and store it in the fridge.
7. Serve and enjoy your spread!

94. CHCOLATE NUT FONDANT

Servings|4 Time|0 minutes

Nutritional Content (per serving):

Cal |245Fat |10g Protein |6g   Carbs| 18g Fibre| 1.5g

Ingredients:

- ❖ 250 grams (1 cup) of cashews
- ❖ 250 grams (1 cup) of walnuts or almonds
- ❖ 250 grams (1 cup) of dried prunes

- ❖ 150 grams (1/4 pound) of butter
- ❖ 250 grams (1 cup) of dates or dried apricots
- ❖ 30 millilitres (2 tbsp) of olive oil
- ❖ A block of 70% dark chocolate

Directions:

1. Start by placing all your ingredients in a blender, but don't add the chocolate.
2. Process your ingredients until they become very well consistent
3. Make sure not to make your ingredients like a nut butter
4. Repeat the same procedure with the dried fruits
5. After processing the fruits, add it to the flour and blend it until you notice your ingredients are very well combined
6. Melt the Chocolate in a heat proof or steel pot with the hot water underneath it.
7. Stir the chocolate until it is completely melted
8. Place your mixture in your soup maker, then add the butter and the oil and mix
9. Pour the chocolate and press the button "smooth" and cook for about 5 minutes
10. Serve and enjoy your chocolate nut fondant!

95. BANANA MILKSHAKE

Servings|2 Time|3 minutes
Nutritional Content (per serving):
Cal |96Fat |7g Protein |6.6g   Carbs| 12g Fibre| 1.3g

Ingredients:

* ❖ 1 banana peeled and cut into slices
* ❖ 300 milliliters of milk
* ❖ 30 grams (3.5 tbsp) of peanut butter

Directions:

1. Place your ingredients in your soup maker
2. Press the button "milkshake" or "smoothie" and set the timer for 3 minutes until you obtain a fluid and creamy texture
3. Enjoy your peanut butter smoothie immediately, decorated with a few peanuts and mint leaves

96. CHOCOLATE MOUSSE

Servings|5 Time|30 minutes

Nutritional Content (per serving):

Cal |101Fat |8g Protein |7g   Carbs| 18g Fibre| 1.2g

Ingredients:

- ❖ 120 grams (1/2 cup) of dark chocolate chips
- ❖ 2 eggs
- ❖ 7 grams (1 tbsp) of vanilla sugar (1/2 package)
- ❖ 20 grams (3 ½ tbsp) caster sugar

- ❖ 60 grams (1/4 cup) of Philadelphia type cream cheese
- ❖ 175 millilitres (1/2 cup) of coffee

Directions:

1. In your soup maker, put the chocolate chips, cheese, eggs, vanilla sugar and sugar.
2. Press the button "smooth" and pour in the hot coffee and cook for about 5 minutes
3. Refrigerate for about 30 minutes
4. Serve and enjoy your chocolate mousse!

97. MANGO AND APPLE COMPOTE

Servings|4 Time|20 minutes

Nutritional Content (per serving):

Cal |225Fat |2g Protein |2.3g Carbs| 27g Fibre| 1g

Ingredients:

- ❖ 2 red apples
- ❖ 2 mangos
- ❖ 2 green apples (Granny Smith)
- ❖ 175 milliliters (1/2 cup) of water
- ❖ 5 grams (1 tsp) of ground cinnamon

Directions:

1. Peel, core and cut the apples into small pieces of the same size.
2. Cut the mangos and put all the apples and mangos in your soup maker.
3. Pour in the water and cinnamon.
4. Press the button "smooth" and cook for about 20 minutes.
5. Serve and enjoy your compote!

98. CUSTAD

Servings|2 Time|15 minutes

Nutritional Content (per serving):

Cal |1503Fat |6g Protein |3g   Carbs| 18g Fibre| 1g

Ingredients:

- ❖ 500 milliliters (1/2 liter) of milk
- ❖ 4 egg yolks
- ❖ 40 grams (1/8 cup) of sugar
- ❖ 15 milliliters (1 tbsp) of vanilla extract

Directions:

1. Put the milk and egg yolks in your soup maker.
2. Add the vanilla and mix very well.
3. Start your soup maker and press the button "smooth" and cook for about 15 minutes.
4. When the timer goes off, turn off your soup maker.
5. Serve and enjoy your custard!

99. PEACH SMOOTHIE

Servings|3 Time|3 minutes

Nutritional Content (per serving):

Cal |223Fat |8.6g Protein |6g Carbs| 13g Fibre| 1g

Ingredients:

- ❖ 250 grams (1 cup) of dried peaches
- ❖ 250 grams (1 cup) of roasted almonds
- ❖ 175 grams (½ cup) of shredded unsweetened coconut
- ❖ 15 millilitres (1 tbsp) of olive oil

- ❖ 250 millilitres (1 cup) of coconut milk
- ❖ grams (2 tbsp) of sugar

Directions:

1. Put the peaches, the almonds, and the coconut into your soup maker.
2. Drizzle in the olive oil and pulse for a few more seconds.
3. Pour in the milk and add the sugar.
4. Press the button "smoothie" and set the timer for 3 minutes.
5. Serve and enjoy your peach smoothie!

100. STRAWBERRY SOUP

Servings|4 Time|5 minutes

Nutritional Content (per serving):

Cal |200Fat |6 g Protein |3 g Carbs| 23g Fibre| 1.6g

Ingredients:

- ❖ 250 grams (1/2 pound) of strawberries
- ❖ 50 grams of icing sugar
- ❖ Juice of a lime
- ❖ 100 grams of white chocolate
- ❖ 150 milliliters of whole whipping cream
- ❖ 1 pinch of white Penja pepper (optional)

Directions:

1. Hull the strawberries and mix them with the icing sugar, the lime juice and the Penja pepper. Pass this preparation through a cheesecloth strainer to obtain a fine and creamy texture.
2. Start your soup maker; then add the strawberries, the whipping cream and the white chocolate.
3. Press the button "smooth"; and cook for about 5 minutes.
4. Serve and enjoy your strawberry soup!

101. HOT CHOCOLATE

Servings|3 Time|8 minutes

Nutritional Content (per serving):

Cal |268Fat |8 g Protein |8g Carbs| 13g Fibre| 0.6g

Ingredients:

- ❖ 175 grams (1/2 cup) of dark pastry chocolate
- ❖ 250 milliliters (1 cup) of milk chocolate
- ❖ ½ liter of semi-skimmed milk (2 cups)
- ❖ 1 Candied lemon or lemon juice

Directions:

1. Crush the dark chocolate or cut it with your hands.
2. Pour into your soup maker with the milk.
3. Choose manual mode to control cooking and grinding time.
4. Grind the chocolate so that it mixes perfectly with the milk.
5. Set the timer to 7 or 8 minutes and press the button "smooth".
6. Pour into a cup and add the candied lemons or 2 tablespoons of lemon juice.
7. Grate the white chocolate over the cup and serve hot.
8. Enjoy your hot chocolate!

102. YOGURT AND BANANA SMOOTHIE

Servings|2 Time|3 minutes

Nutritional Content (per serving):

Cal |106Fat |7 g Protein |10g Carbs| 17g Fibre| 1 g

Ingredients:

- ❖ 2 yogurts
- ❖ 2 bananas
- ❖ 250 milliliters of milk (1 cup)

Directions:

1. Peel the bananas and cut them into slices.
2. Pour the bananas in your soup maker
3. Pour in the milk and the yogurt
4. Press the button "smoothie" and set the timer to 3 minutes
5. Once ready
6. Add a few ice cubes and blend again
7. Serve and enjoy your smoothie!

Thanks for Reading

We hope you that you benefited and enjoyed this book. And if you found this material helpful to you, please feel free to share it with your friends. You can help others find this material too by leaving feedback that will help us continue writing books you enjoy.

Printed in Great Britain
by Amazon

25279329R00071